# DATE DUE

# Mayo Clinic
# on Alzheimer's Disease

**Ronald Petersen, M.D., Ph.D.**

Editor in Chief

**MASON CREST PUBLISHERS**

Philadelphia, Pennsylvania

*Mayo Clinic on Alzheimer's Disease* provides in-depth discussion of the current knowledge of the disease and its relationship to other forms of dementia. This book also contains practical explanations of treatment and caregiving. Much of this information comes directly from the experience of physicians, psychiatrists, neurologists and allied health care professionals at Mayo Clinic. This book can assist your understanding of Alzheimer's and help guide your treatment decisions. *Mayo Clinic on Alzheimer's Disease* does not endorse any company or product. MAYO, MAYO CLINIC, MAYO CLINIC HEALTH INFORMATION and the Mayo triple-shield logo are marks of Mayo Foundation for Medical Education and Research.

© 2002 Mayo Foundation for Medical Education and Research

Hardcover Library Edition Published 2002
Mason Crest Publishers
370 Reed Road
Suite 302
Broomall, PA 19008-0914
(866) MCP-BOOK (toll free)

First printing

1 2 3 4 5 6 7 8 9 10

Library of Congress Cataloging-in-Publication Data on file at the Library of Congress

ISBN 1-59084-542-0

Photo credits: Cover photos and the photos on pages 1, 25, 63, 91 and 159 are from PhotoDisc.

Printed in the United States of America

## About Alzheimer's disease

Alzheimer's disease is the most common form of dementia. Dementia is a loss of intellectual and social abilities that is severe enough to interfere with daily functioning. This loss occurs in people with Alzheimer's because – for reasons unclear – healthy brain tissue degenerates, causing a steady decline in memory and other cognitive skills.

Perhaps as many as 4 million Americans have Alzheimer's, a disease that usually develops in people age 65 or older. The number of people with Alzheimer's is expected to quadruple in the next 50 years as more and more individuals live into their 80s and 90s.

Although there is no cure or surefire way to prevent Alzheimer's, scientists have made great progress in understanding the disease. Physicians are now able to diagnose the condition at much earlier stages and treatments are available that help improve the quality of life for people with Alzheimer's. Within these pages, you'll find the information you need – based on the expertise of Mayo Clinic -- to better understand this complex disease and the latest advances in research.

## About Mayo Clinic

Mayo Clinic evolved from the frontier practice of Dr. William Worrall Mayo and the partnership of his two sons, William J. and Charles H. Mayo, in the early 1900s. Pressed by the demands of their busy practice in Rochester, Minn., the Mayo brothers invited other physicians to join them, pioneering the private group practice of medicine. Today, with more than 2,000 physicians and scientists at its three major locations in Rochester, Minn., Jacksonville, Fla., and Scottsdale, Ariz., Mayo Clinic is dedicated to providing comprehensive diagnoses, accurate answers, and effective treatments.

With this depth of medical knowledge, experience and expertise, Mayo Clinic occupies an unparalleled position as a health information resource. Since 1983 Mayo Clinic has published reliable health information for millions of consumers through award-winning newsletters, books and online services. Revenue from the publishing activities supports Mayo Clinic programs, including medical education and research.

## Editorial staff

**Editor in Chief**
Ronald Petersen, M.D., Ph.D.

**Managing Editor**
Kevin Kaufman

**Copy Editor**
Judy Duguid

**Proofreading**
Miranda Attlesey
Donna Hanson

**Editorial Research**
Anthony Cook
Deirdre Herman
Michelle Hewlett

**Contributing Writers**
Rachel Haring
Briana Melom

**Creative Director**
Daniel Brevick

**Design**
Craig King

**Illustration and Photography**
Brian Fyffe
Christopher Srnka

**Indexing**
Larry Harrison

## Contributing editors and reviewers

Bradley Boeve, M.D.
Richard Caselli, M.D.
Dennis Dickson, M.D.
Christopher Frye
Yonas Geda, M.D.
Neill Graff-Radford, M.D.
Michael Hutton, Ph.D.
Robert Ivnik, Ph.D.
Clifford Jack, Jr., M.D.
Kris Johnson, R.N.
David Knopman, M.D.
Angela Lunde

Joseph Parisi, M.D.
Maria Shiung
Glenn Smith, Ph.D.
Eric Tangalos, M.D.
David Tang-Wai, M.D.
Robert Witte, M.D.
Steven Younkin, M.D., Ph.D.

# Preface

People frequently associate aging with the loss of mental functions, such as memory and judgment, and the onset of difficult behaviors, such as depression and anxiety. These experiences aren't necessarily a part of normal aging. They may be, in fact, signs of dementia. This book focuses on Alzheimer's disease, the most common form of dementia.

Explaining Alzheimer's disease is not an easy task. For one thing, there's so much we don't know about the disease, including its cause and how to halt or delay its progress in the brain. For another thing, understanding Alzheimer's requires some in-depth knowledge of the brain's complexities. The first part of this book attempts to explain the disease clearly and succinctly using the expertise and experience of Mayo Clinic. We believe this material is essential to understanding and coming to terms with events that occur as the disease develops.

This book also provides you with a broad overview of caregiving, along with helping to guide you to the most authoritative resources. In addition, we offer the Quick Guide for Caregivers, a handy, easily accessible reference covering many urgent concerns.

In preparing this book, we would like to acknowledge two individuals who were instrumental in launching and fostering Alzheimer's disease research at Mayo Clinic: Emre Kokmen, M.D., and Leonard Kurland, M.D., D.P.H.

*Ronald Petersen, M.D., Ph.D.*
Editor in Chief

# Contents

# Part 3: Treating Alzheimer's disease

# Part 4: Caregiving for Alzheimer's disease

# Part 1

## Aging and dementia

# Chapter 1

# Normal aging and Alzheimer's disease

Considering the constant wear and tear on your body over the years, is there any wonder at the changes that result from aging? Yet it often comes as a surprise when your muscles and joints can't do what they used to or your mind doesn't seem as agile as it once was. Aging often catches people unawares. Although this complex process called growing old occurs over many years, to some it seems to happen overnight.

> **What is the secret of the trick?**
>
> **How did I get so old so quick?**
>
> **Ogden Nash**
> Preface to the Past

The real issue may be not the rate at which people age but rather the differences in the way they age. Why does everyone seem to grow old so differently? There are 60-year-olds who look and act younger than 60 — and others who seem considerably older than their age. How can some people remain relatively vibrant and active into their 90s or even 100s while others of the same age have been unable to function and care for themselves for many years? Some of the differences are due to a combination of genetics, lifestyle and environment — with a measure of luck thrown in.

But the answer may also have to do with other processes such as disease. Heart disease, stroke, high blood pressure, diabetes, or dementia can be the cause of severe physical and mental impairment. Unfortunately, the effects of disease in older adults are sometimes passed off as a normal part of aging, and the underlying cause remains undiagnosed. Some of these conditions are potentially treatable, but others are not. This book deals with one of the most devastating and untreatable disorders among older adults — Alzheimer's disease (AD).

## Is something wrong with me, or am I just getting old?

Your initial concerns about Alzheimer's disease may stem from the misgivings and anxiety that result from your experiences with memory loss. Alzheimer's disease is a condition that occurs when there is a breakdown in the brain, in particular when there is a loss of communication among brain cells. Clear communication among brain cells is vital for the brain to function properly. If your brain's networking capabilities deteriorate, cognitive skills — such as your ability to think, reason and remember — are affected or lost.

Unfortunately, a commonly held notion about growing old is that aged brains are incapable of reasoning and remembering. It's true that as you age, you may expect a certain amount of forgetfulness and may require more time to respond to complex problems. But there is often uncertainty about whether symptoms such as these can mean something more serious than aging. At other times these symptoms are simply accepted or ignored.

The effects of Alzheimer's disease are more severe than anything caused by normal aging. Alzheimer's is an abnormal condition, like cancer or diabetes, and its causes are as yet unknown. The disease develops in a slow, concealed manner that can obscure the full extent of its damage to the brain. Unfortunately, its course is unrelenting and irreversible. To date, there is no cure, although scientists are accomplishing much in the way of understanding and diagnosing the condition and treating its symptoms.

When should you become concerned about your forgetfulness? Everyone forgets things from time to time, but memory loss caused by Alzheimer's is persistent and becomes more severe over time. The disease progresses to eventually affect your language, judgment, understanding and ability to focus attention. Your behavior

## Forgetfulness

The forgetfulness that sometimes accompanies aging is usually a sign that your brain functions are slowing down. You simply need more time to remember a name or the task you had set out to do. But this doesn't prevent you from living a full and productive life. You're aware that you're forgetful and may acknowledge it to others with a joke or a shrug.

People with memory loss due to something other than normal aging, such as Alzheimer's disease, may have a very different experience. In many cases, they feel that something's not quite right but are unable to pinpoint what's bothering them. Rather than call attention to a memory lapse, they may behave as if everything is fine.

may change, and you may become aggressive, overly anxious or depressed or may even wander from home. Eventually, Alzheimer's disease destroys your ability to perform even the simplest of tasks, such as eating and getting dressed.

While Alzheimer's disease primarily affects adults over the age of 60, this does not mean that AD is an inevitable result of getting older or that all older adults will eventually display its signs and symptoms. It is believed that a potential for the disease may develop over many years, and individuals exhibit symptoms only later in life. In very rare cases, Alzheimer's affects people in their 30s and 40s. You can learn to live with occasional memory lapses. But persistent and gradually more severe memory loss is of greater concern and may be a cause to visit your doctor.

## The aging of America

In the last century, technological advances and improvements in sanitation, public health and preventive medicine have helped people live longer lives. In 1900, the average life expectancy was 47 years. Currently, life expectancy is around 76 years. In fact, older adults are one of the fastest growing segments of the population.

## How long will you live?

| Year | Life expectancy at birth | | Additional years after 65 | |
|------|------|--------|------|--------|
| | **Male** | **Female** | **Male** | **Female** |
| 1900 | 46.4 | 49.0 | 11.4 | 11.7 |
| 1920 | 54.5 | 56.3 | 11.8 | 12.3 |
| 1940 | 61.4 | 65.7 | 11.9 | 13.4 |
| 1960 | 66.7 | 73.2 | 12.9 | 15.9 |
| 1980 | 69.9 | 77.5 | 14.0 | 18.4 |
| 2000 | 73.2 | 79.7 | 15.8 | 19.3 |

Timing, as they say, is everything. If you were a baby in 1900 you could expect to reach your mid- to late 40s. If you survived the onslaught of childhood diseases and you reached 65, you'd probably live until your mid-70s. On the other hand, if you were born in 2000 and you live to age 65, you can expect to live until your early to mid-80s.

Source: Office of the Chief Actuary, Social Security Administration

Today approximately 35 million Americans are over the age of 65. The U.S. Census Bureau projects that by the year 2050, close to 82 million people will be in this age group.

As more and more people live into their retirement years, diseases such as Alzheimer's, which tend to develop later in life, are becoming more common. Studies consistently show that the number of people with Alzheimer's disease (the prevalence of AD) rises sharply with each year of age, doubling every 5 years after the age of 65. Estimates of how many people currently have Alzheimer's range from 2 million to 4 million people. More women are affected than men. All the reasons for this pattern are not clear, although one obvious reason is that women generally live longer than men.

Currently around 360,000 new cases of Alzheimer's disease (the incidence of AD) are reported each year in the United States. Because the population of older adults is increasing in size, however, scientists estimate that the number of new cases of Alzheimer's reported annually also will increase. Some studies project a quadrupling of the number of people living with the disease in the next 50 years, resulting in a significant increase in health care costs.

While the emotional burden of Alzheimer's is difficult to determine, the financial costs can be calculated — and they're staggering. Different studies suggest that the average annual cost of caring for someone with Alzheimer's ranges from $27,000 to $47,000. Experts estimate that the total annual cost of Alzheimer's care on a national level runs in the billions of dollars.

The problem has not gone unnoticed. Research on Alzheimer's disease has become a national priority supported by the U.S. government. Investigators are focusing not only on finding the causes and risk factors associated with Alzheimer's, but also on identifying the disease in its earliest stages and improving methods of treatment and caregiving. Studies suggest that if treatment were to provide even a 2-year delay in the onset of the disease, it could reduce the expected number of people with Alzheimer's in 50 years by almost 2 million.

## Projected number of Americans living into their 100s 2000 to 2050

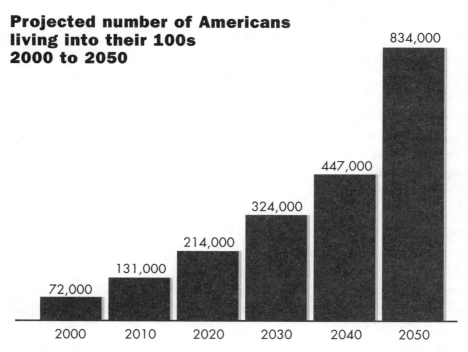

Source: J.C. Day, 1996, Population Projections of the United States by Age, Sex, Race, and Hispanic Origin. U.S. Bureau of Census, Current Population Reports, P25-1130, U.S. Government Printing Office, Washington, D.C.

# Toward a better understanding of aging

Studying Alzheimer's and other diseases that can affect you as you get older has allowed investigators to learn more about the normal process of aging. The fundamental question that some scientists strive to answer is how someone ages in the absence of disease. Is it possible to characterize the course of "normal" aging?

As an indication, the Baltimore Longitudinal Study of Aging has published general statements about how people typically age:

- Your heart grows slightly larger, and maximum oxygen consumption decreases.
- Your systolic blood pressure increases.
- Your muscle mass and hand grip decline.
- Your maximum breathing capacity declines.
- Your brain sustains loss and damage of nerve cells.
- Your bladder loses capacity, leading to more frequent urination and incontinence.
- Your kidneys become less efficient in removing wastes from the bloodstream.

Remember that this information only describes what happens on average to groups of people. It doesn't predict exactly how aging will happen to you. How you age depends on your own individual combination of genetics, lifestyle and environment, topped off by any influence of the disease process.

Much age-related change occurs at the most fundamental level — within your cells. Cells are the basic building blocks of the tissues and organs that make up your body. As you age, certain cells lose some of their function. Cell membranes change, making the process of receiving nutrients and getting rid of toxic waste more difficult. Tissues tend to become stiffer, making organs, blood vessels and air passageways more rigid.

Does aging affect cognition? Researchers are still trying to answer that question. Your brain is made up of billions of cells. As you age, the number of brain cells gradually decreases, leading to a loss or shrinking of brain mass, a process called atrophy. The loss is distributed unevenly throughout the brain, with some parts affected more than others. Although it is difficult to trace cognitive problems directly to these physical changes, some loss of memory and rea-soning skills may be expected among older adults. Sensory skills, such as touch, taste, hearing, vision and sense of smell, become less efficient as nerve-cell communication slows.

But scientists also know that many of the changes that are some-times labeled as senility are not inevitable with age. Many older adults remain mentally alert and active and as intelligent as they ever were. Their concerns usually involve a slowing down in the retrieval of information. On the other hand, severe memory loss, confusion, personality changes and the inability to perform routine tasks are known collectively as dementia and result from abnormal brain processes, not age. Alzheimer's disease is the most common cause of dementia.

## Toward a better understanding of Alzheimer's

After receiving the diagnosis of Alzheimer's disease, former Presi-dent Ronald Reagan wrote a letter to the American people saying he hoped that disclosing his own diagnosis might enhance aware-ness of the disease everywhere. As a matter of fact, the world has achieved a greater understanding of Alzheimer's in the last 10 years than in the 50 years preceding them. Even now, scientists are continuing to uncover new findings about the brain and about Alzheimer's at an unprecedented rate.

The chapters that follow provide you with current knowledge of this condition — how Alzheimer's disease changes the brain, how these changes affect the person who develops Alzheimer's, and how doctors are able to diagnose it. This book also presents the latest theories about Alzheimer's causes and course of development, and describes what's being done to find ways to both effectively treat and prevent this disease.

More important to you, perhaps, is practical advice on how to cope with Alzheimer's here and now, including how to accept a diagnosis and move on, transition into the role of caregiver, deal with challenging behaviors, maintain relationships and care for yourself in the midst of caring for others. In the middle section of the book, you'll find the Quick Guide for dealing with a variety of situations, ranging from exercise and nutrition to handling anxiety. You'll see that although Alzheimer's disease is a serious challenge, it is one that many people around the world face on a daily basis, successfully and meaningfully.

## Senility and dementia

*Senility* is a word that is often considered synonymous with the word *dementia*. With the term *senile dementia*, the two words are even used together. Is there a difference between the two words?

The term *senile* comes from the Latin word *senilis*, meaning "old man." The dictionary defines senile as exhibiting a loss of mental faculties associated with old age — in other words, those cognitive or behavioral problems considered characteristic of some older adults. In many respects, the term is outdated.

*Dementia* is a medical term indicating a syndrome — a collection of signs and symptoms — that involves declining intellectual and social abilities that are more severe than what would occur through aging. The signs and symptoms of dementia include severe memory loss, disorientation and changes in personality. Many disorders can cause dementia, including Alzheimer's disease.

In the past, what we now know to be dementia was often labeled senility by medical professionals. Degeneration of the brain was thought to be simply the result of getting old. Today scientists know that although dementia may be associated with growing old, it is not a part of the normal process of aging.

# Chapter 2

# How the brain works and what can go wrong

W ith dedication and zeal akin to that of the astronomers and cosmologists who study the universe, scientists are pursuing the secrets of the mind. The human brain has been measured, scanned, tested, dissected, described and analyzed countless times. But each mystery that has been resolved only seems to uncover other questions and riddles about the workings of the brain. Advances in science and technology have provided so many new insights into this vital part of the human body that the U.S. Congress labeled the 1990s as the Decade of the Brain. Despite these breakthroughs, the brain remains a source of fascination and wonder.

> The human brain weighs only 3 to 4 pounds but contains about 100 billion neurons [nerve cells]. Although that extraordinary number is of the same order of magnitude as the number of stars in the Milky Way, it cannot account for the complexity of the brain.
>
> **Gerald D. Fischbach, M.D.**
> *Mind and Brain*

In Chapter 1 you learned that Alzheimer's disease involves a breakdown in the communication that goes on among billions of brain cells. In order to understand how this breakdown occurs, it's helpful to know how a normal brain works. In this chapter, you look at various structures of the human brain and learn some of their main functions. You also see how the parts of the brain can malfunction and how the resulting damage may cause dementia.

## The brain and nervous system

The brain controls virtually all of your body's activities, from basic instincts of survival to elaborate intellectual analysis and creative thought. It organizes and shapes your emotions. It monitors and directs your body functions and physical actions. Your brain is protected by the bony shell of your skull and cushioned by layers of membrane. An intricate network of blood vessels supplies the food and oxygen it needs. Chemicals within the nerve cells of your brain produce electric signals. These impulses are transmitted along pathways known as circuits. The circuits are the means by which you receive, process, store, retrieve and transmit information.

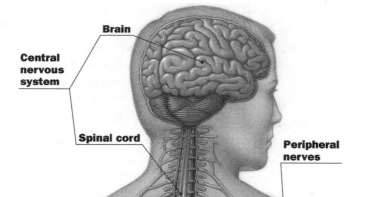

**The nervous system**

Brain

Central
nervous
system

Spinal cord

Peripheral
nerves

Together with your spinal cord, the brain makes up your central nervous system. Extending from your spinal cord are nerves that branch out through your body, all the way to the tips of your fingers and toes. This network is called the peripheral nervous system. These nerves are constantly gathering information from both inside and outside your body and sending messages to your brain describing what they've found and asking how they should respond.

Your brain receives hundreds of messages from this network of nerves. As your brain interprets and prioritizes the messages, relevant bits of information are sent to different parts of your brain for memory storage. When interpretation is complete, which can be a split-second process, the brain shoots back instructions that tell your fingers, legs, mouth, heart or any other part of your body how to respond.

By rapidly processing, sorting, filing and responding to this continuous barrage of incoming messages, your brain gives meaning to the world around you. The manner in which your brain performs these tasks, which is different from the way any other person's brain functions, makes you the unique person you are.

## A tour of the functional brain

Your brain is made up of various structures, and each structure has a variety of responsibilities and tasks to perform. In a normal, healthy brain, these structures work together in an efficient, coordinated and incredibly complex fashion.

The basic structures of the brain include the brain stem, the cerebellum and the cerebrum. The brain stem, located at the base of the brain, is responsible for some of the most basic functions you need

**Lobes of the brain**

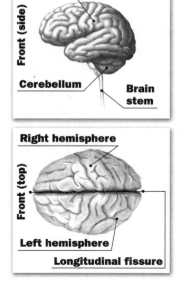

Front (side)

Cerebrum

Cerebellum   Brain stem

Front (top)

Right hemisphere

Left hemisphere

Longitudinal fissure

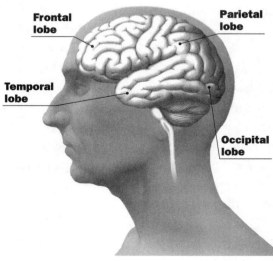

Frontal lobe

Parietal lobe

Temporal lobe

Occipital lobe

to survive, such as breathing and controlling heart rate. The cerebellum, which sits at the back of the brain stem, is responsible for balance and movement.

The cerebrum, resting on top of the brain stem, is the largest structure of the human brain and perhaps the most recognizable due to its heavily folded appearance. The outer surface of your cerebrum is a layer of tissue less than a quarter of an inch thick. Grayish-brown and wrinkled looking, this layer is the cerebral cortex, or what is commonly called your gray matter. The cerebral cortex is where most of your intellectual operations take place: thinking, reasoning, analyzing, organizing, creating, decision making and planning for the future. The grooves and folds of the cortex allow a greater surface area to fit inside the skull, thus increasing the amount of information that can be processed. Underneath the cerebral cortex is white matter, which plays an important role in the transmission of nerve impulses among the various structures of your brain.

The cerebrum is divided into left and right hemispheres separated by a deep fissure. Putting your two fists together in front of you can give you a rough picture of what your cerebrum looks like. The two hemispheres are connected by a thick band of nerve cell fibers called the corpus callosum.

Each hemisphere is subdivided into four lobes, and each lobe directs different activities. The frontal lobe in each hemisphere, located directly behind your forehead, is associated with personality, problem solving, abstract thought and skilled movement. Behind the frontal lobe is the parietal lobe, which receives sensory information such as pain, taste and touch. This lobe supports your visuospatial abilities, which allow you to orient yourself and navigate within your surrounding environment. The temporal lobe is situated roughly behind your temple at the side of your forehead. This area is vital for hearing and language comprehension and is involved with perception and memory. At the back of each hemisphere is the occipital lobe, which is primarily responsible for your vision and is therefore also called the visual cortex.

The limbic system is located in the internal regions of the brain and is associated with your emotions and motivation (see page C1

**The functional brain**

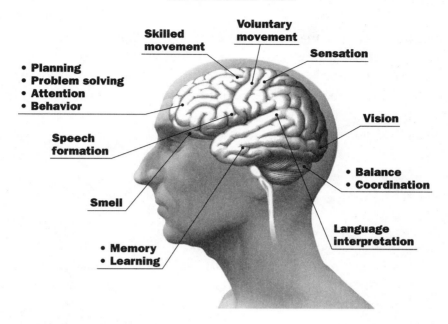

in the color section). It is closely connected to your frontal and temporal lobes. The system is composed of several structures that play a role in processing all of the sensory information bombarding your brain and in regulating vital body systems. The structures include:

- The hypothalamus, which controls body functions such as eating, sleeping and sexual behavior, maintains body temperature and chemical balance, and regulates hormones
- The amygdala (uh-MIG-duh-luh), which governs such emotions as anger and fear and triggers your response to danger, whether that response is confronting a situation or fleeing it (commonly called the flight-or-fight response)
- The hippocampus (hip-o-KAM-pus), which plays a crucial role in your memory system, sorting and sending new bits of information to be stored in appropriate sections of your brain and recalling them when necessary

Another internal structure of the brain, but not a part of the limbic system, is the thalamus. The job of the thalamus is to filter and prioritize information from your senses and relay messages to and from various parts of your brain.

# Cognitive functions

The term *cognition* comes from the Latin word *cognoscere*, which means "to know." It makes sense, then, that your cognitive skills are the ones that enable you to know things. Perception, reasoning, attention, judgment, memory and intuition are all important cognitive skills. The many aspects of cognition are essential functions of your brain.

## Making memories

Memory involves your ability to store information about objects, experiences and events and to recall and use that information for your immediate needs or future plans. But there isn't a central warehouse in your brain where all memory is processed and stored. Your hippocampus sorts and parcels up sensory information and integrates each bit in its proper storage network in many parts in the brain. For example, the sound of a favorite song may be stored in the temporal lobes, which contain the auditory areas of your brain. Your knowledge of the lyrics, on the other hand, may be held in the language and visual areas of the frontal, temporal, parietal and occipital lobes. To recall a single memory may require the reassembly of bits of information from many parts of your brain.

For a memory to be stored for a long time, it must go through a process called consolidation. Say you're learning to play the piano. You strike a skinny black key and the sound of it vibrates briefly in your ears. That brief millisecond of recognition is your sensory memory in action. Then your teacher points to a squiggle on a piece of paper in front of you and says, "That's the note for an E flat." You hit the key again. The sound of the note and the information you received from your teacher are now registered in your short-term memory.

If you go away and never play that note again, the information you learned will likely be forgotten and you will probably not remember what an E flat sounds like. If, however, you practice

Although in the preceding section, cognitive activities such as memory were associated with specific parts of the brain, most mental activities in fact rely on multiple regions of the brain. For example, the hippocampus may be the central switchboard of your memory system, but the system also requires the participation of the frontal cortex and the temporal cortex. And almost every part of the brain is involved in memory storage. Likewise, your ability to focus attention, which enables you to select objects or occurrences in your

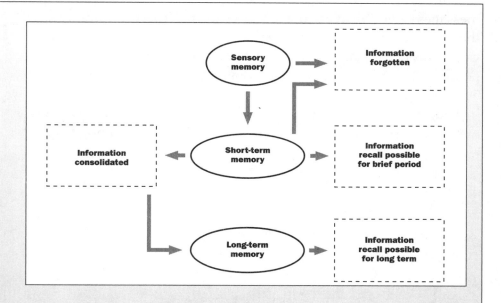

regularly, associating the note on the paper with the key you are playing, this information will pass into your long-term memory. Consolidation of memories generally requires attention, repetition and associated ideas. Information that has been consolidated is not as easily forgotten as that in short-term memory.

Emotionally charged events can also be registered in your long-term memory, although they don't need the repetition required of learned information. Many people will forever remember where they were and what they were doing at the moment of a calamity. An example would be the attacks on the World Trade Center and the Pentagon on Sept. 11, 2001.

environment that are most relevant to you — and ignore what is not relevant — depends heavily on the frontal lobes. But your thalamus, brain stem, other structures of your limbic system and other parts of your cerebral cortex also play vital roles.

## Neurons and cell communication

The basic unit of your brain and nervous system is a nerve cell called a neuron. Neurons allow different parts of your body to communicate. They do so by generating electric impulses — messages — and relaying the impulses to and from your brain and the rest of your body. Surrounding the neurons are neuroglia cells that act as bodyguards — they protect, nourish and support the neurons. The human brain contains about 12 billion neurons and 50 billion neuroglia cells.

Each neuron is made up of a cell body, which contains a nucleus and other structures essential to neuron function. Extending from

**Neuron Structure**

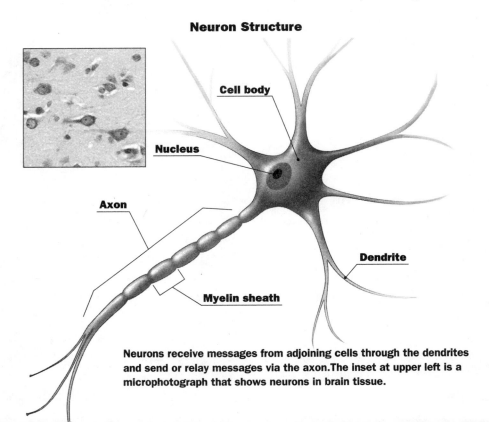

Neurons receive messages from adjoining cells through the dendrites and send or relay messages via the axon. The inset at upper left is a microphotograph that shows neurons in brain tissue.

the cell body are branches called dendrites that receive incoming messages from other neurons. Also extending from the cell body is a single, larger branch called an axon. The axon carries outgoing messages from the cell body to other cells. Interconnected in this way, neurons communicate in an efficient, lightning-quick fashion.

Wrapped around most axons is a white, fatty substance called myelin. Myelin helps insulate the axon and speeds up the transmission of messages. Myelin-covered axons, which appear white, are found in the white matter of the cerebrum.

In order to send an impulse (the message), a neuron must be stimulated by something. This can range from a prick on your finger to a funny scene in a movie to an incoming impulse from another neuron. Within the neuron, an electric impulse travels through the cell body to the tip of the axon, where there are tiny sacs containing neurotransmitters — chemicals that act as data messengers (see page C2 in the color section). The arrival of the impulse signals the release of neurotransmitters into a synapse, which is the space between the axon and an adjoining cell. In the synapse, the neurotransmitters bind to receptors on the receiving cell. The membrane of the receiving cell is altered in a way that re-creates the impulse, and the process begins again.

Once the neurotransmitters have done their job, they're either destroyed or returned to their cell of origin, where they may be reused. In this way, a message is passed from neuron to neuron until the impulse travels to its intended destination, which could be a part of the brain, an organ such as your heart or lungs, or any one of your muscles.

Neurons stay healthy by converting nutrients found in circulating blood, such as oxygen, into energy. *Metabolism* is a word for all the chemical reactions that continuously take place in your body to help keep you alive. One type of metabolic reaction breaks down substances to release the energy you need to live. Another type of metabolic reaction builds up substances your body needs to repair or renovate cells so that they can function properly. Proteins play an important role in maintaining cells and tissues. For example, special proteins called enzymes help to speed up reactions and thus assist your metabolism.

## How things go wrong

Like a finely tuned machine, your brain and nervous system depend on a harmonious balance among all parts for efficient operation. But as described earlier, the aging process brings about changes in your brain that can upset this balance. Nerve cells die each day, and new ones aren't regenerated to replace them. The cerebellum, the cerebrum and the hippocampus suffer considerable cell loss as a result of aging (affecting memory, balance and movement, for example), although the brain stem, the thalamus and the hypothalamus seem to be affected less (maintaining many basic survival functions). The synapses that allow cells to communicate disappear. The circuits of certain neurotransmitters become blocked, further inhibiting communication. Your brain shrinks in size and weight. These changes may result in slight forgetfulness and a slowing down of your cognitive function. For example, problems remembering names or finding the right word are increasingly common with age.

Although these effects of aging are troublesome and may require lifestyle changes, they don't necessarily incapacitate you. Severe impairment of your mental functions, which often denies you your independence and the ability to care for yourself, is frequently the result of a neurodegenerative disorder. As the word implies, *neurodegenerative* involves the degeneration of neurons — but many more than what occurs in normal aging. There are many different neurodegenerative disorders, including Alzheimer's disease, Parkinson's disease, Huntington's disease and frontotemporal dementia. Some disorders may be hereditary, and others are sporadic — meaning there may be only a single occurrence within a family. The cause of many of these disorders is unknown, but their development is often characterized by a buildup of defective proteins in the brain. Healthy cells can generally dispose of defective proteins. But with a neurodegenerative disorder, this protein material accumulates, clumps together and begins to interfere with the normal function of nerve cells.

The different neurodegenerative disorders can affect very different structures of the brain. Disorders such as Parkinson's disease impair

## Protein buildup: A common link

A characteristic shared by many neurodegenerative disorders is the abnormal buildup of certain proteins in the brain. These proteins do not come from your diet but rather are produced by your body itself. Proteins are compounds that perform many vital tasks in your body. There are thousands of different kinds of proteins that do different things. Most scientists believe that the buildup of certain proteins is toxic to neurons and suspect that it is at least one cause of the signs and symptoms in people who have these disorders. Different types of proteins are associated with different disorders:

| Disorder | Protein |
|---|---|
| Alzheimer's disease | Amyloid |
| Parkinson's disease | Alpha-synuclein |
| Creutzfeldt-Jakob diseases | Prions |
| Huntington's disease | Huntingtin |
| Frontotemporal dementia with Parkinson's disease (FTDP-17), Progressive supranuclear palsy, Pick's disease | Tau |

Researchers are currently investigating ways to reduce, eliminate or prevent the buildup of these proteins. The hope is that such action may be the basis for treating the disease in question.

muscle movement and coordination and cause tremors. A disorder such as Alzheimer's affects a person's memory and cognition, very often accompanied by challenging behaviors. There may also be problems with speech and language comprehension. Someone who exhibits this particular group of symptoms may receive a diagnoisis of what's known as dementia.

## Signs and symptoms of dementia

Dementia is a progressive decline in intellectual and social abilities that affect your daily functioning. It's a result of abnormal brain processes, not age. However, studies do indicate that dementia becomes more common as people grow older. An estimated 4 percent to 8 percent of people over age 65 may have moderate to severe dementia. For those over age 80, up to 20 percent may have some form of dementia.

In fact, dementia is a syndrome — a collection of signs and symptoms occurring together — and not the name for a single disorder. Many conditions can cause dementia. Some forms are caused by specific neurologic or medical diseases and may be treatable. In other forms, such as Alzheimer's disease, the causes are unknown and treatment can't halt their progress.

It is often difficult to recognize the early signs and symptoms of dementia. The signs and symptoms will vary from individual to individual, depending on the person's genetic makeup, lifestyle, cultural background and personal life experiences. Some of the common characteristics of dementia include:

- Severe memory loss
- Confusion
- Inability to formulate abstract thoughts
- Difficulty concentrating
- Difficulty carrying out routine or complex tasks
- Personality changes
- Paranoid or bizarre behavior

Conditions such as high fever, dehydration, vitamin deficiency and poor nutrition, thyroid problems, bad reactions to medicines and minor head injuries can all cause changes in the brain and affect cognitive functions. But many of these conditions are temporary, sudden and reversible. Being depressed, feeling lonely or bored and having to cope with late-life changes also can leave a person feeling disoriented.

On the other hand, persistent forgetfulness and confusion can be signs of Alzheimer's disease, small strokes (vascular dementia) or any of a number of other brain disorders known to cause dementia. If you notice these symptoms in yourself or in a loved one, it's important not to brush them off as simply "getting old." Talk to your doctor. He or she can help you sort things out. If the condition is reversible, you can get appropriate treatment. Even if it's not, an early diagnosis is still the best diagnosis. When treatment of a condition such as Alzheimer's is begun early, there's a greater chance that you can more effectively manage the disease.

**Causes of dementia**

Alzheimer's disease 56%

Vascular dementia or vascular causes 14%

Frontotemporel dementia 8%

Parkinson's disease and/or Lewy body dementia 10%

Multiple causes or other causes 12%

This pie chart is a rough approximation that gives you a general sense of dementia's many complex causes.

## Conditions that mimic dementia

Some conditions produce signs and symptoms that can be mistaken for dementia, particularly in older adults. One such condition is depression. In casual usage, the term *depression* may describe a temporary low mood that comes from a bad day or a bad feeling. As a medical term, *depression* denotes a serious illness that may cause difficulty in remembering, thinking clearly and concentrating. Other symptoms may include an ongoing sense of sadness and despair and an inability to enjoy activities that once brought you pleasure. It affects how you feel, think, eat, sleep and act.

Depression may result from life changes such as retirement or the death of a spouse. Sometimes, depression occurs in conjunction with dementia. In such cases, the deterioration of your emotions and intellect can be more extreme.

Another condition that may mimic dementia is delirium — a state of mental confusion, disordered speech and clouded consciousness. These signs and symptoms may be mistaken for those of dementia, but there are important differences. One is the abruptness with which delirium signs and symptoms develop. Someone who exhibits sudden disorientation, agitation, loss of consciousness or hallucinations is likely to have delirium rather than dementia. Sometimes, emergency medical treatment of delirium is vital because the underlying cause may be a serious medical illness such as bacterial meningitis. Delirium can be common in older adults who have lung or heart disease, long-term infections, poor nutrition, medication interactions or hormone disorders. Someone with dementia also can develop delirium, often from a complication such as a urinary tract infection.

The point to remember is that whether they occur alone or in combination with dementia, both depression and delirium are treatable conditions. If you think you might be exhibiting signs and symptoms of either, see your doctor. The sooner the condition is diagnosed, the sooner you may find relief and start to feel better.

# Part 2

*Understanding
Alzheimer's disease*

# Chapter 3

# What is Alzheimer's disease?

Alzheimer's disease (AD) is the most common cause of dementia. It primarily affects adults in their 60s or older. Its development is unrelenting and irreversible. Alzheimer's gradually robs a person of intellect and memory and the ability to reason, learn and communicate. The disease changes a person's personality and impairs judgment. It ultimately destroys a person's ability to perform simple, routine tasks or even to care for himself or herself. The course Alzheimer's takes may run anywhere from 2 to 20 years after the first signs appear, although death often occurs in about 8 to 10 years. It's worth emphasizing that the course the disease will take is highly variable from person to person. A caregiver shouldn't assume that death is imminent for a loved one who has had the disease for 8 years.

## How Alzheimer's disease affects the brain

Alzheimer's disease affects the brain by destroying its basic component, the neuron. Neuron loss occurs first in the hippocampus, the central switchboard of your memory system. That's why memory loss is often associated with the early stages of Alzheimer's. There may also be disorientation and the loss of spatial memory — which is the perception of where objects or places are located in relation to

### Parts of the brain affected in the early stage of Alzheimer's

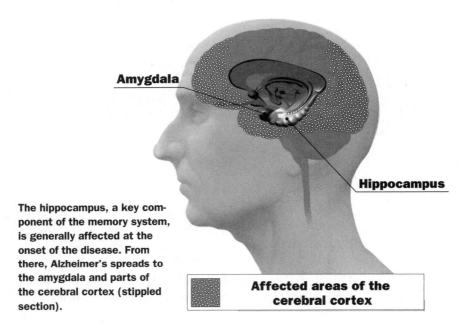

**Amygdala**

**Hippocampus**

The hippocampus, a key component of the memory system, is generally affected at the onset of the disease. From there, Alzheimer's spreads to the amygdala and parts of the cerebral cortex (stippled section).

**Affected areas of the cerebral cortex**

each other, such as the location of your bathroom in relation to the bedroom or kitchen.

From the hippocampus, Alzheimer's spreads to the frontal, parietal and temporal lobes of the cerebral cortex. Besides the hippocampus, the disease also attacks other parts of the limbic system, including the amygdala. As neurons are damaged and destroyed in these areas, there is damage to other cognitive functions such as language skills and the ability to plan, make judgments and perform simple tasks. Since the limbic system is the part of your brain that influences instincts, drives and emotions, neuron loss in this area may explain the aggressive behavior and paranoia often seen in people with Alzheimer's.

In addition, Alzheimer's causes a loss of nerve cells within the brain at a location called the basal nucleus of Meynert. This area is rich in the neurotransmitter called acetylcholine (uh-set-ul-KOE-leen). As noted earlier, neurotransmitters are the chemical messengers that carry impulses from neuron to neuron. Acetylcholine is important for the formation and retrieval of

## Neurotransmitter loss associated with Alzheimer's disease

| Neurotransmitter | Primary function |
|---|---|
| Acetylcholine | Attention, learning and memory |
| Dopamine | Physical movement |
| Glutamate | Learning and long-term memory |
| Norepinephrine | Emotional response |
| Serotonin | Mood and anxiety |

memories, and damage to the basal nucleus causes a sharp drop in acetylcholine levels. In addition to causing a loss of acetylcholine, Alzheimer's disease also affects the levels of other important neurotransmitters.

Eventually, Alzheimer's affects many parts of the brain. As more neurons degenerate, more synapses — points of communication between cells — are destroyed. With the loss of nerve cells, the brain mass shrinks. The person

**Acetylcholine in the brain**

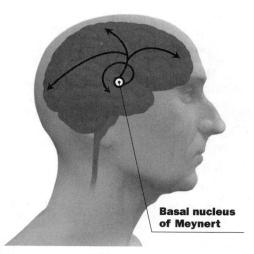

**Basal nucleus of Meynert**

Brain cells that produce acetylcholine are located along well-defined pathways in the cerebral cortex. The basal nucleus of Meynert is involved in memory and learning.

with Alzheimer's starts to lose some of his or her functions, including the ability to communicate, recognize familiar faces and objects, and control behavior and basic physical urges, such as the need to eat or to urinate. In the final stages of Alzheimer's disease, most people are bedridden and completely dependent on others for care.

# Plaques and tangles

Two distinctive characteristics of Alzheimer's disease are amyloid plaques and neurofibrillary tangles. Researchers believe the uncommonly high number of these protein deposits may in some way play a role in the destruction of neurons in the brain.

**Amyloid plaques.** Amyloid plaques are abnormal aggregations of tissue that consists mainly of a protein called beta-amyloid. The plaques can be found between the living nerve cells. These plaques are believed to form early in the disease process, before neurons begin to die and the symptoms of memory loss and dementia become obvious.

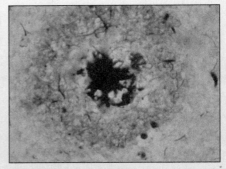

A dense core of tissue lies at the center of many amyloid plaques. Surrounding the core is an area of inflammation.

**Neurofibrillary tangles.** *Neurofibrillary* refers to tiny filaments or fibers inside nerve cells. Neurofibrillary tangles form when threads of a protein called tau start to twist. Normally, tau serves a useful function, working to uphold the structure of a neuron. In people with Alzheimer's, tau proteins undergo chemical alterations that cause them to twist. Lacking sufficient support, the structure of the cell collapses.

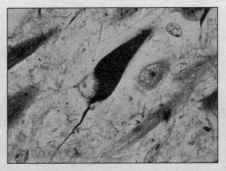

The dark mass on this image is the collapsed structure of a neuron. Tau protein within the cell has twisted, undoing the cell structure.

Scientists are faced with unraveling a thorny problem: Do plaques and tangles cause Alzheimer's, or are they a result of the disease? Plaques and tangles have been observed in the brains of people who show no signs and symptoms of dementia. But in people with Alzheimer's, the plaques and tangles occur in much greater number.

## Mild cognitive impairment:
## A precursor to Alzheimer's disease?

Researchers are attempting to clarify the boundaries between what we consider the effects of normal aging and the onset of Alzheimer's disease. Presumably, with respect to cognitive functions, there's a

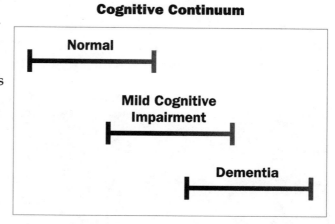

**Cognitive Continuum**

Normal

Mild Cognitive Impairment

Dementia

continuum between "normal" and early signs of the disease. This transitional area in the continuum has been labeled mild cognitive impairment (MCI).

In general, the thinking and reasoning skills of people with MCI stay sharp and their activities of daily living are normal, but memory impairment — especially of recently acquired knowledge — is greater than what one would expect for their age. Over time, the mental and functional abilities of people with MCI seem to decline at a faster rate than that of those individuals without MCI. But the decline is less rapid than that of those with a diagnosis of mild Alzheimer's disease.

Study results suggest that MCI places you at increased risk for Alzheimer's — and, in fact, the condition may be a precursor of AD. People with MCI may have as much as a 50 percent chance of developing Alzheimer's within 4 years after their initial diagnosis. At the same time, it's important to stress that although the risk is increased, not everyone with MCI will develop Alzheimer's.

This new category of memory loss may help doctors more accurately identify the earliest signs and symptoms of Alzheimer's (see pages C4 - C5 in the color section). Research may then focus on a treatment to delay the onset of the disease, thus allowing people with MCI to live independently longer.

# How Alzheimer's disease progresses

People with Alzheimer's experience the disease in different ways from one another. The differences depend on many factors including age, personality, physical health, family history and cultural and ethnic backgrounds. The rate at which changes occur, and the severity of these changes, also will vary from person to person.

**Brain atrophy and Alzheimer's**

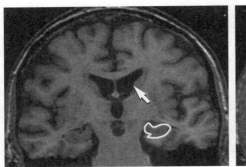 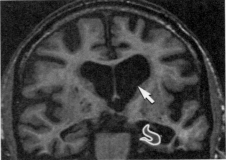

These magnetic resonance images (MRIs) of the brain compare a person without Alzheimer's (left) with a person in the moderate stage of the disease (right). The progression of Alzheimer's is indicated on the right by a hippocampus that is noticeably shrunken (circled in white) and interior cavities of the brain that have enlarged and filled with cerebrospinal fluid (indicated by arrow).

Nevertheless, certain indicators are common in almost everyone with Alzheimer's as the disease progresses. Using these indicators as symptomatic benchmarks, medical professionals describe the development of Alzheimer's in stages ranging from mild to severe. Some experts divide this range into three stages, others into four or more. What distinguishes one stage from another is the appearance of or a change in the various indicators, in terms of cognition (how a person thinks), behavior (how a person acts) and function (how a person performs basic tasks of living).

In this book, three stages are used to categorize Alzheimer's disease: mild, moderate and severe (see page C3 in the color section). The description of each stage is only a general one, which may not fit each person's circumstances exactly. Some of the signs and symptoms that are described may overlap from one stage to the next. Other signs and symptoms may never occur in some people.

## Mild Alzheimer's

Early warning signs of Alzheimer's are often subtle, making it difficult to recognize that something is wrong. Even if people recognize changes, they may not associate the changes with a health problem. Many people in the early stage seem less aware and less concerned about their problems. This lack of awareness may itself be a symptom of Alzheimer's disease. Some of the earliest signs and symptoms include:

- Asking the same questions repeatedly
- Getting lost in conversations and having problems finding the right word
- Not being able to complete familiar tasks, such as following a recipe
- Having problems with abstract thought
- Not remembering recent events
- Misplacing items in inappropriate places, such as putting a wallet in the refrigerator
- Undergoing sudden changes in mood or behavior for no apparent reason
- Showing an inability to concentrate or take initiative
- Having less interest in his or her surroundings
- Showing an indifference to personal appearance or normal courtesies to others
- Feeling disoriented as to time and place
- Becoming lost while driving on familiar streets

In the mild stage of Alzheimer's, a person may still be working and trying to go about business as usual. The difficulties may be passed off as stress, lack of sleep, fatigue or simply a part of getting older. The person may try to compensate for memory problems by sticking to familiar things, places and routines and not entering into new or strange situations. A growing awareness of memory loss may lead to feelings of anger, frustration and helplessness. It's not unusual for a person to take these emotions out on others. Depression also is common at this stage, a condition that should be evaluated and treated as soon as possible.

# What does it feel like to have Alzheimer's?

Mayo Clinic's Alzheimer's Disease Research Center asked a group of people who received a diagnosis in the mild stage of Alzheimer's about their experiences. Answers are surprisingly revealing. Some are philosophical, others pragmatic.

## What changes have occurred in your life as a result of the memory loss?

"Loss of independence. It doesn't feel right to become more dependent on others by letting them get the idea that you can't do anything. I give in and let others take over completely. You lose out when you let others take over. We need to slow down so I can stay involved."

"Fear. You hear it's so debilitating and that gets you down."

"When they hear Alzheimer's, people back up like you've got a 'disease.' Almost like you should be ashamed. Like they are wondering if it's catchy or if maybe she's going to die soon."

"Expectations others have for me are often too high or too low. I can't keep up with my spouse. It's quicker and easier to let my spouse take over."

"I need to be reminded of tasks or activities."

"I don't recognize places when we go for drives. That scares me."

"It takes me much longer to remember why I went into a room."

"I need to work at a slower pace. People around me seem like they are on a merry-go-round — going faster and faster. I can't keep up. I want to stay active, but I need to take more time to do things."

## Moderate Alzheimer's

In this stage, the warning signs of Alzheimer's disease have become more evident. These changes may alert family members or friends that something is wrong. The person may not only be experiencing memory loss but also be having difficulty exercising good judgment and thinking clearly. If there had been any reluctance to see a doctor before, these concerns may prompt a doctor visit now. A diagnosis of Alzheimer's is often made at this stage. Some signs and symptoms of the moderate stage include:

- Forgetting to turn off appliances such as the iron or the stove
- Consistently forgetting to take medications
- Having difficulty with tasks involving calculation and planning, such as balancing a checkbook and paying bills, going grocery shopping or planning dinner
- Having difficulty with tasks that require skilled movements such as tying shoelaces or using utensils
- Losing the ability to communicate, including reading and writing
- Exhibiting behaviors such as aggressiveness, outbursts of anger, or withdrawal
- Behaving inappropriately in public
- Feeling increasingly agitated and restless, particularly at night
- Sleeping for excessively long periods of time or hardly sleeping at all (Some people may sleep 10 to 12 hours at night and still nap during the day, others may sleep only 2 to 4 hours at night.)
- Having hallucinations or delusions

A diagnosis of Alzheimer's at any stage is important because it not only explains why these distressing changes are occurring but also gives everyone a direction in which to plan for the future. This can be a trying time for anyone thrust into the unanticipated role of caregiver, whether it be a spouse, child or other family member or friend. A new perspective must be brought to bear on the relationship between the caregiver and the person who just received a diagnosis of Alzheimer's.

## Where is my wife?

This haunting question was asked of a wife who assumed a care-giving role for her husband. She describes the changes that occurred in their relationship this way:

"It is heartbreaking for your spouse not to know you. But I have learned not to let it get to me. I tell my husband that his wife will soon be back or, if he persists, that she has gone to visit family.

At times, he tells me that his wife has gone to visit family, and I should sleep in the guest room. Well, I tell him that this bed is just like mine and I would sleep better in it. He will get in bed and sleep at the farthest edge. But before he goes to sleep, he reaches over and holds my hand and kisses me goodnight."

— Edna L.

### Severe Alzheimer's

In the final stage of Alzheimer's disease, the signs and symptoms worsen to a point where the person is no longer able to think or reason. The essential tasks of living, such as eating or going to the bathroom, require assistance. The person's personality may have changed completely. Some of the signs and symptoms at this severe stage include:

- Having little or no memory
- Having difficulty speaking and understanding words
- Expressing little or no emotion
- Grasping objects or people and not letting go
- Having difficulty recognizing others and perhaps not even recognizing himself or herself when looking in a mirror
- Needing assistance for all personal care, including using the toilet, bathing, dressing, eating and moving around
- Experiencing frequent incontinence
- Feeling increasingly weak and being susceptible to infections
- Having difficulty chewing and swallowing and because of that, losing weight

A person in the final stage of Alzheimer's may eventually become bedridden. His or her body systems may be severely weakened, which will often increase the risk of developing other health problems. The impact of these added health problems is frequently more severe for a person with Alzheimer's than for someone without the disease. As a result, the cause of death is rarely Alzheimer's itself, but more often a secondary infection such as pneumonia. As noted earlier in the chapter, death occurs, on average, about 8 to 10 years following the initial diagnosis of Alzheimer's by a doctor.

## Conditions that may accompany Alzheimer's

A number of disorders can occur at the same time that Alzheimer's is developing in the body. The symptoms of any of these conditions can obscure or complicate a diagnosis of Alzheimer's. They may also hasten or increase the severity of mental decline. The fact that many of these conditions are treatable makes an early diagnosis of them important. Some of the conditions that commonly coexist with Alzheimer's include depression, anxiety and sleep disorders.

**Depression.** Depression is the most common condition that accompanies the various forms of dementia. Among people with a diagnosis of Alzheimer's, nearly 30 percent to 40 percent experience significant depression at some point during the course of the disease. It's especially common during the early stages of Alzheimer's when social isolation, diminishing mental and physical abilities and a loss of independence often occur. Although brief periods of discouragement and apathy may be natural in such cases, prolonged despondency is not.

Research indicates that chronic feelings of sadness or worthlessness among people with Alzheimer's are emotional reactions to the awareness of their own mental decline. On the other hand, major depression may be associated with the biological changes of Alzheimer's in the brain. Some studies suggest that the symptoms of depression, such as apathy and a lack of motivation, may be among the earliest signs of AD. Other studies point to the idea that depression may increase your chances of developing Alzheimer's.

Although it may be difficult to know if a person is depressed, you might look for some of the following signs:

- Loss of appetite
- Sleep disturbance
- Lack of energy and initiative
- Feelings of low self-esteem
- Irritability and anxiety
- Poor concentration

If the person seems easily distressed and he or she wasn't that way before, that also might be a sign of depression. If you observe any of these changes, tell your doctor. Even if it isn't depression, it's important to identify any underlying reasons for distress.

Diagnosing depression in a person with Alzheimer's can be especially challenging. This is due, in part, to the person's growing inability to describe how he or she feels. Another complicating factor is that many adults have been socialized to think that it's OK to be physically sick but not OK to admit to feelings of sadness or depression. Experts encourage caregivers to take part in the doctor visits to provide a more complete picture of the person's moods.

**Anxiety.** Anxiety involves an extreme sense of fear about some future event, real or imagined. Research indicates that anxiety occurs in approximately 40 percent to 70 percent of people with Alzheimer's. Anxiety and depression often occur together. The symptoms of anxiety may include:

- Fearfulness
- Apprehension
- Excessive worry
- Anger
- Agitation
- Fidgeting or pacing
- Restlessness

Anxiety seems to be closely associated with many troublesome behaviors that may occur in someone with Alzheimer's. These include wandering, inappropriate sexual conduct, hallucinations, verbal threats and physical abuse. These behaviors are frequent reasons for putting someone in a nursing home. Treating anxiety effectively might improve the symptoms of the person with Alzheimer's and, in turn, reduce the stress and fatigue that affect the caregiver.

**Sleep disorders.** Disturbed sleep patterns are common among people with Alzheimer's, particularly in the later stages of the disease. The form these disturbances take varies greatly. Some people may sleep more than they ever did before, up to 16 hours a day.

Others may sleep less, perhaps only 2 to 4 hours a night. Furthermore, the cycle of sleep and wakefulness may become reversed. Restlessness and wandering at nighttime are common.

Other sleep disorders include sleep apnea, restless leg syndrome and periodic limb movements during sleep. Some people may seem to "act out" their dreams. People with Alzheimer's may also experience loud snoring, episodes of snorting or gasping, a creepy-crawly sensation in their legs (especially at night) or nightmares. If someone exhibits any of these signs and symptoms, you should discuss them with your doctor. Most of these sleep disorders are treatable, and successful treatment can improve cognition, mood and quality of life.

Such disturbances may also affect the caregiver's sleep patterns. In such cases, it's important that the caregiver find a way to obtain necessary rest, so he or she does not become sleep deprived.

## Alzheimer's and other forms of dementia

Alzheimer's disease sometimes occurs in conjunction with other diseases that cause dementia. This can present a challenge to the doctor attempting a diagnosis. Your doctor will carefully study all of the signs and symptoms to distinguish between Alzheimer's and other dementia-causing conditions.

**Vascular dementia.** Approximately 15 percent to 20 percent of all people with dementia in fact have Alzheimer's combined with another common condition called vascular dementia. Vascular dementia, also known as multi-infarct dementia, results from an interruption of blood flow to the brain, either from a blockage of arteries or from a series of strokes. Mental ability deteriorates step by step with each additional stroke. Not surprisingly, a major risk factor is a history of strokes. Other risk factors include high blood pressure and high cholesterol levels. Paralysis, vision loss and difficulty with speaking and using language are commonly found in people suffering from vascular dementia. Often, the onset of vascular dementia is abrupt, but occasionally the disease progresses slowly, making it difficult to distinguish from Alzheimer's.

**Lewy body dementia and dementia associated with Parkinson's disease.** Lewy bodies are protein deposits that progressively destroy brain cells. When Lewy bodies are widespread throughout the brain, a person may have symptoms similar to those of both Alzheimer's disease and Parkinson's disease. Concentration problems and other dementia symptoms often appear first. Later, the stiff or shaky movements associated with Parkinson's may occur. The person also may suffer from visual hallucinations. The cause of Lewy body dementia is unknown, but recent studies indicate that it is a common cause of dementia.

As many as 30 percent to 40 percent of people with Parkinson's disease eventually develop dementia. Parkinson's is a crippling disease characterized by stiffness of the limbs, tremors, difficulty with walking and speech impairment. Lewy bodies often appear in damaged regions of the brains of people with Parkinson's disease. And some people with Alzheimer's also will have these particular protein deposits.

**Frontotemporal dementia.** Frontotemporal dementia (FTD) is a rare brain disorder characterized by disturbances in behavior and personality, language impairment and eventually memory loss. The name comes from the fact that the frontal lobes and temporal lobes of the brain are most susceptible. One of the causes of this dementia is Pick's disease, which is characterized by abnormal structures within the affected cells that cause the neurons to swell. Because of the disruptive, inappropriate behavior associated with this condition, a person is often evaluated by a psychiatrist.

## Advancing our understanding

Scientists have identified the signs and symptoms of each stage as Alzheimer's progresses through the brain. They have identified conditions, including other forms of dementia, which may exist concurrently with Alzheimer's. The subject of the next chapter is the causes of this insidious disease, a vital and still unanswered question.

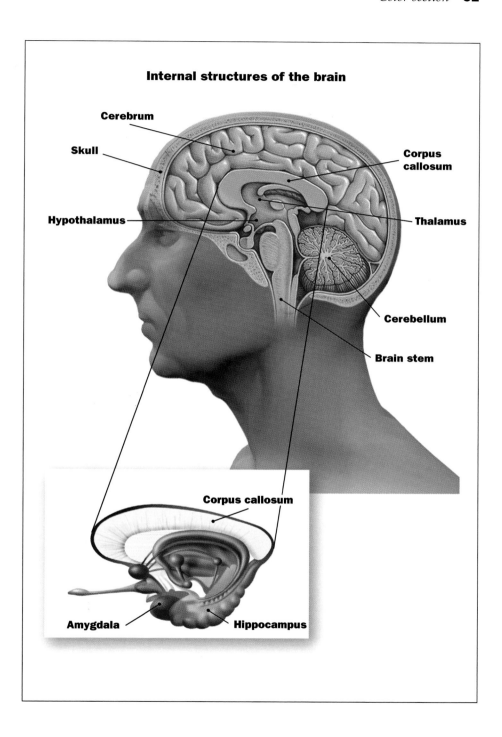

Internal structures of the brain

## How neurons communicate

Neurons communicate by exchanging electric impulses. When one neuron prepares to communicate with another neuron, the impulse travels through the body of the sending nerve cell to the tip of its axon.

Axon of sending
nerve cell

Synapse

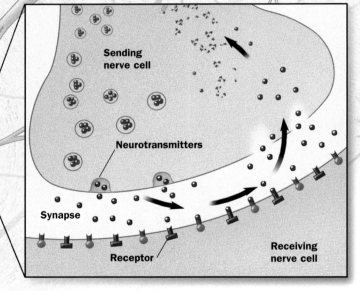

Sending
nerve cell

Neurotransmitters

Synapse

Receiving
nerve cell

Receptor

Receiving
nerve cell

At the tip of the axon are tiny sacs containing neurotransmitters, which are chemical messengers. The arrival of the impulse signals a release of the neurotransmitters into the synapse, which is the space between the axon of the sending neuron and an adjoining cell.

In the synapse, the neurotransmitters bind to receptors on the receiving cell. This alters the activity of the receiving cell in a way that re-creates the impulse. In this way, a message is passed from neuron to neuron until the impulse travels to its intended destination.

# Brain atrophy and Alzheimer's disease

The stages of Alzheimer's disease are evident in this sequence of magnetic resonance images (MRIs). These images are sagital sections, as seen directly from the side of the head.

The four MRIs show four different individuals with differently sized and shaped brains. Nevertheless, the widening grooves and fissures of the cerebral cortex indicate progressively severe brain atrophy and loss of brain mass.

**Sagital section**

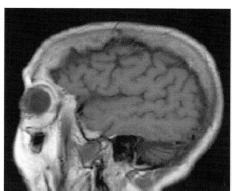

**Normal**

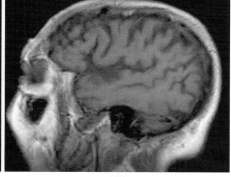

**Mild Alzheimer's**

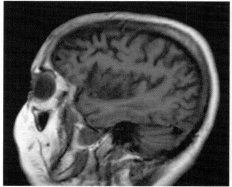

**Moderate Alzheimer's**

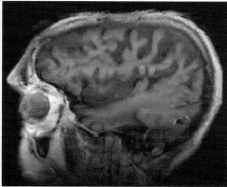

**Severe Alzheimer's**

## The onset of Alzheimer's disease

Alzheimer's disease attacks the brain by destroying its most basic component, the neuron. At the onset of Alzheimer's, neuron loss often occurs first in the hippocampus. Then the amygdala and sections of the cerebral cortex are affected. Cognitive functions such as memory and language are impaired early in the disease process. Moods and emotions become increasingly unstable. Eventually, Alzheimer's affects just about every part of the brain.

### Brain structure

This sequence of MRIs reveals shrinkage of the hippocampus in the brain during the transition from normal to mild cognitive impairment to mild Alzheimer's. On these images it's also possible to see that the interior cavities of the brain enlarge as the disease advances. The shrinkage of the hippocampus explains why memory loss is often one of the first warning signs of Alzheimer's. The inset that accompanies each MRI is an enlarged view of the left hippocampus.

**Normal brain**

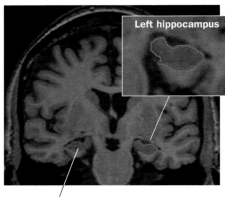

Left hippocampus

Right hippocampus

Coronal section

### Brain function

This sequence of PET scans shows a reduction of brain activity during the transition from normal to mild cognitive impairment to mild Alzheimer's. This is indicated by a diminishing of the intense white and yellow areas on the images from left to right. The PET scan of mild Alzheimer's also shows an increase of blue and green colors, indicating reduced brain activity.

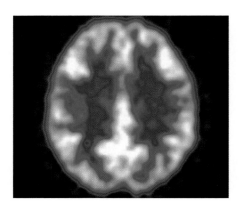

Axial section

Imaging technology, including magnetic resonance imaging (MRI) and positron emission tomography (PET), makes changes in the structure and function of the brain visible to researchers.

- MRIs provide a clear picture of brain anatomy and structure. The images below are coronal sections, as seen directly from the front of the head.
- PETs show the intensity of brain activity. White and yellow areas on the scans indicate high activity while blue and green areas indicate low activity. The PET images below are axial sections, as seen directly above the head.

### Mild cognitive impairment

### Mild Alzheimer's disease

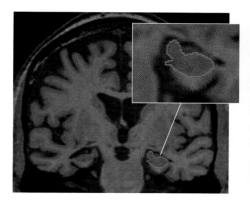
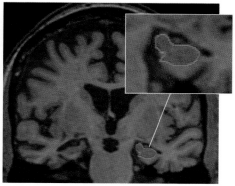

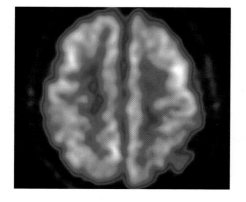
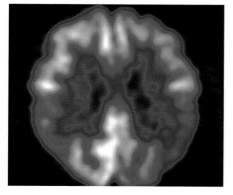

## The formation of amyloid plaques

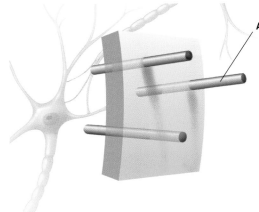

Amyloid precursor protein

The amyloid precursor protein (APP) is lodged partly inside and partly outside a nerve cell membrane. From this position, APP is clipped off outside the cell membrane by three different enzymes: alpha-secretase, beta-secretase and gamma-secretase.

### Normal processing of APP

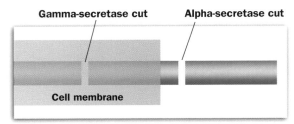

Gamma-secretase cut          Alpha-secretase cut

Cell membrane

When alpha-secretase and gamma-secretase clip APP, the resulting fragments seem to dissolve easily within the brain.

### Abnormal processing of APP

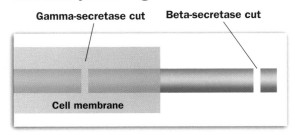

Gamma-secretase cut     Beta-secretase cut

Cell membrane

When beta-secretase and gamma-secretase clip APP, they often produce long fragments called beta-amyloid 42. Beta-amyloid 42 does not dissolve easily and accumulates in the brain to form plaques.

### Amyloid plaque

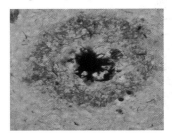

The dark, irregular spot in this microphotograph is a dense core of material at the center of the amyloid plaque. The discoloration surrounding the core indicates inflammation.

## The formation of neurofibrillary tangles

Tau protein helps to uphold the structure of a neuron. It does so by keeping microtubules in place. Microtubules are intracellular structures that provide cell support and serve as conduits for materials moving within the cell.

Sometimes, chemical changes inside the neuron alter the tau protein. This causes the tau to contort and detach from the microtubules, and form the neurofibrillary tangles. The microtubules no longer stay firmly in place. Cell structure collapses and the neuron dies.

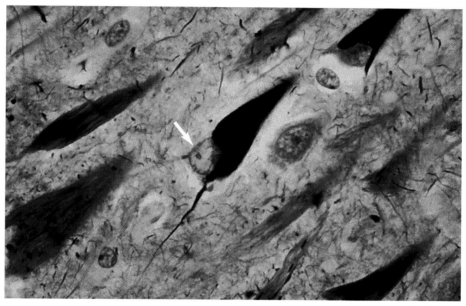

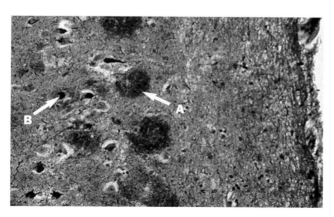

The dark, solid masses in the microphotograph above are the collapsed structures of neurons. In the central mass, a cell nucleus is still evident in the collapsed structure (indicated by the arrow).

A sample of brain tissue showing an accumulation of amyloid plaques (arrow A) and neurofibrillary tangles (arrow B) in a person with Alzheimer's disease.

## Cells, chromosomes and genes

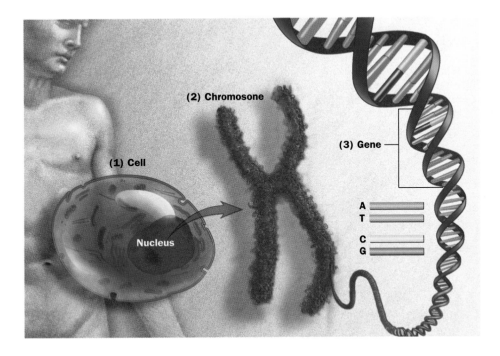

(1) Your body is made up of cells — about 100 trillion of them. Within the nucleus of each cell — except the egg and sperm cells — are two sets of 23 chromosomes, 46 chromosomes in total.

(2) Each chromosome is made up of a tightly coiled strands of deoxyribonucleic acid (DNA). The structure of DNA resembles a twisting ladder held together by chemical rungs made of paired nucleotide bases.

The nucleotide bases that form the rungs of the DNA ladder are adenine (A), thymine (T), cytosine (C) and guanine (G). Adenine always pairs up with thymine (A/T) and cytosine always pairs up with guanine (C/G).

(3) The DNA in your chromosomes is arranged into short segments called genes. Each gene consists of sets of paired nucleotide bases bracketed by beginning and ending markers.

Each gene contains instructions for the cell to produce a chemical, usually a protein with a specific task to do. Many different kinds of proteins are essential for the development and maintenance of your body.

Sometimes there is an unexpected change in the DNA, which may affect a gene, which in turn may affect how a protein is made or how a protein functions. This change is called a mutation. Mutations may cause disease, including Alzheimer's.

# Chapter 4

# What causes Alzheimer's disease?

T he causes of Alzheimer's disease (AD) are a much-pondered mystery. Ever since Alois Alzheimer identified the characteristic plaques and tangles of the disease in the early 20th century, researchers and scientists have ardently pursued hundreds of different leads in a quest to understand and combat its destructive nature. The pace of this research has accelerated in recent years, with scientists turning up new information almost daily.

Investigating the causes of Alzheimer's is like piecing together a jigsaw puzzle. The problem is, no one knows what the finished product will look like. Furthermore, the jumbled pieces seem to come from several different and seemingly unrelated puzzles. Until the final picture is complete, the hope is that identifying and understanding more about the factors involved in Alzheimer's disease will lead to new treatment and prevention strategies.

## Early-onset and late-onset Alzheimer's

Before we examine some of the factors involved in Alzheimer's, it's important to draw a distinction between two forms of the disease. Scientists classify Alzheimer's disease into early-onset and late-onset forms, using the age of 65 as a dividing line. People younger

## Inheritance patterns in Alzheimer's disease

Researchers use age 65 to identify people with Alzheimer's as having either early-onset or late-onset forms of the disease. But researchers also recognize a different kind of breakdown into familial and sporadic forms of Alzheimer's. Familial means that multiple members of the same family have been affected by the disease, and sporadic means that only one person in the family has Alzheimer's.

Why is there a need for these categories? One reason is the different patterns of inheritance they reveal. For example, the early-onset familial form of Alzheimer's is rare but strongly hereditary. The more common late-onset form of the disease, be it familial or sporadic, doesn't have as clear an inheritance pattern.

Of course, these are not exclusive categories, and the distinctions among them can be blurred. In fact, it's possible for the late-onset sporadic form to affect more than one member of a family and thus appear familial, while a familial form may affect only one family member and appear sporadic.

than 65 who develop Alzheimer's have the early-onset form. Although this group is relatively small in number, it spans a wide age range. There are rare instances where people in their 30s have developed Alzheimer's.

People who get Alzheimer's when they are 65 or older have late-onset AD, the more common form. The symptoms of both forms are much the same, although in some instances of early onset there is a more rapid rate of physical and mental decline. A big distinction between the two forms of Alzheimer's is in the way the early-onset form impacts the life of a middle-age person — who may be working and still have parental responsibilities. The impact of the late-onset form on an older adult establishes very different needs and priorities.

For both forms of Alzheimer's, scientists do know that the disease is complex and think it's very likely caused by a combination of genetic and environmental factors. Approximately 30 percent of all people with Alzheimer's have a family history of dementia, indicating that genes play a role. Genetic risk factors aren't the whole story, however. Researchers are also investigating environmental factors that may contribute to the development of Alzheimer's. Scientists aren't sure how all of these events are related or what other factors are yet to be identified and explained, but a broader view of the disease is emerging.

## Genetic factors affecting Alzheimer's disease

Much of the research on Alzheimer's has been and remains focused on the genetic factors surrounding the disease. For basic information about genetics, see page C8 in the color section. A greater understanding has been gained from this genetic research and is providing valuable insight into the complex cascade of events that forms the disease process.

Certain genetic mutations — unexpected changes in single genes or in sections of chromosomes — are known to cause a small number of early-onset forms of AD. Researchers have evidence that other undiscovered genes and genetic mutations may influence Alzheimer's, whether directly or indirectly.

Something that all of the genes and genetic mutations known to cause Alzheimer's share is the abnormal processing and degradation of the beta-amyloid precursor protein. The abnormal processing generally results in an excessive production of beta-amyloid fragments. When the fragments do not dissolve, they bunch together to form the abundant plaques found in the brains of people with Alzheimer's. More and more, scientists are becoming convinced that the increased accumulation of beta-amyloid in the brain is, if not a direct cause of dementia, a vital and necessary step in the process. A closer look at each gene may help to explain how beta-amyloid may contribute to Alzheimer's.

### Amyloid precursor protein
Amyloid precursor protein (APP) is associated with the cell membrane, the thin outer covering of a cell. The gene that produces this protein is located on chromosome 21 of a person's DNA. The normal

function of APP isn't clear, but studies indicate that it plays a role in the growth and the survival of neurons. Mutations of APP cause a rare form of Alzheimer's disease.

APP is sometimes called a membrane protein because it becomes lodged partly inside and partly outside the cell membrane, like a pin stuck in a cushion. From this position, APP is clipped off outside the cell membrane by a type of enzyme called a protease (PRO-tee-ays). An enzyme is a type of protein that speeds up reactions. Scientists have known for some time that three proteases are involved in this process, and even though they aren't sure of the exact identity of all of these enzymes, the scientists have labeled them alpha-secretase (SI-kre-tays), beta-secretase and gamma-secretase.

## Genes associated with Alzheimer's

| Gene | Chromosome |
|---|---|
| Amyloid precursor protein (APP) | 21 |
| Presenilin 1 (PS1) | 14 |
| Presenilin 2 (PS2) | 1 |
| Apolipoprotein E (APOE ε4) | 19 |

All three enzymes clip APP from the cell membrane. When alpha-secretase and gamma-secretase cut APP, the resulting fragments seem to dissolve fairly easily within the brain (see page C6 in the color section). Beta-secretase and gamma-secretase cut the protein as well. They produce longer fragments called either beta-amyloid 40 or beta-amyloid 42 (because they're made up of either 40 or 42 amino acids). Beta-amyloid 42 does not easily dissolve and is "stickier" than beta-amyloid 40. Beta-amyloid 42 accumulates with other fragments to form the Alzheimer's plaques.

The mutations of the APP gene that are associated with Alzheimer's are located on the part of the APP that's sticking outside the cell membrane and close to the secretase clipping sites. This suggests that these mutations cause the formation of more beta-amyloid in total or more of the beta-amyloid 42 version. Either case would lead to the creation of more plaques.

### Presenilin protein

Mutations of two different presenilin proteins, presenilin 1 (PS1) and presenilin 2 (PS2), are known to cause Alzheimer's disease. The gene for the PS1 protein is located on chromosome 14. The gene for the PS2 protein is located on chromosome 1. More than 30 different mutations of these proteins cause early-onset Alzheimer's disease. A parent who has any one of these known presenilin mutations has a high chance of passing it on to his or her child. Each child has a 50 percent chance of inheriting the abnormal gene and develop-ing the disease. This closely links presenilin to familial forms of Alzheimer's.

Studies show that PS1 and PS2 mutations increase the level of beta-amyloid 42 in the brain — the sticky version of beta-amyloid that produces the amyloid plaques. Scientists have suspected for quite some time that the PS1 protein is the gamma-secretase enzyme involved in clipping APP.

### Apolipoprotein

Before being linked to Alzheimer's disease, the apolipoprotein E (APOE) gene was already known in the medical community for its part in carrying blood cholesterol through the body. There are three alleles, or variants, of APOE — named ε2, ε3 and ε4. Unlike the APP, PS1 and PS2 genes, it's not a mutation of APOE that plays a role in Alzheimer's but one of the naturally occurring variants of the gene — the ε4 allele. And while APP, PS1 and PS2 lead to the early-onset form of Alzheimer's, inheriting one or two of the APOE ε4 alleles increases your chance of developing the late-onset form of Alzheimer's. It may also lower the age of onset — usually years earli-er than non-APOE ε4-related forms of Alzheimer's. Research shows that APOE ε4 is associated with an increase in the amount of beta-amyloid in the brain, but exactly how this happens is debated. Some researchers suspect that although the ε3 and ε2 alleles are effective at dissolving beta-amyloid from the brain, the ε4 allele is not as effective.

## Genetic factors under investigation

Researchers are studying chromosome 12 — in particular, the alpha-2-macroglobulin gene that's found on chromosome 12 — as a possible source for another late-onset risk factor. Chromosome 10 also is being studied. Recently, three groups of researchers determined separately and through different methods that a late-onset Alzheimer's-related gene appears to reside on chromosome 10. It is thought that this gene may also affect the processing of the beta-amyloid protein.

## Theories of what may cause Alzheimer's disease

The efforts to uncover genetic links to Alzheimer's have produced encouraging results. These results are helping scientists focus on specific factors that affect Alzheimer's, if not actually triggering the disease process.

### Beta-amyloid and plaques

The study of various genetic mutations suggests that the processing of beta-amyloid and the formation of plaques play important roles in the development of Alzheimer's. Some researchers believe these are essential stages of the Alzheimer's disease process. The factors that support this hypothesis include the following:

- All known early-onset familial forms of Alzheimer's are accompanied by a substantial increase in the level of beta-amyloid protein in the brain.
- The aggregation of beta-amyloid into plaques occurs early in the disease process, before symptoms appear.
- Over time, the number of plaques increases as the disease develops in the brain.
- People with Down syndrome, who by the nature of their condition carry an extra copy of all or part of chromosome 21 and thus three APP genes (instead of two), frequently develop Alzheimer's later in life.
- A mutation of the gene that produces the amyloid precursor protein itself causes Alzheimer's.

The question that remains unanswered within the beta-amyloid theory is whether the plaques are the direct cause of cognitive decline. Are they the driving force behind the onset of Alzheimer's? Initial studies on mice whose genes have been altered to produce Alzheimer's-like plaques (known as transgenic mice) are supportive of this notion. And if so, would removing excess beta-amyloid from the brain or halting overproduction of beta-amyloid eliminate the cognitive and behavioral symptoms of AD? These are issues that scientists hope to clarify.

**Characteristic features of Alzheimer's**

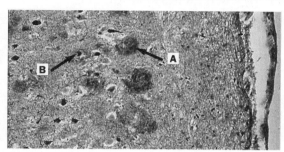

This microphotograph of brain tissue shows the accumulation of beta-amyloid plaques (arrow A) and neurofibrillary tangles (arrow B) in a person with Alzheimer's disease.

Meanwhile, other researchers are studying alternative explanations. Although beta-amyloid aggregation may be a first step in the development of Alzheimer's, other changes may occur early in the process. Prominent changes in the brain include the accumulation of neurofibrillary tangles — a characteristic that appears to have a strong relationship to the severity of Alzheimer's symptoms. In addition, inflammatory response, oxidative stress and a disruption of calcium levels leading to nerve cell death are important mechanisms that may contribute to the disease.

## Tau and neurofibrillary tangles

Neurofibrillary tangles are caused by twisted tau proteins inside nerve cells. Tau normally helps uphold the structure of a neuron. When the tau protein breaks down, the cell structure collapses (see page C7 in the color section). Tangles may be found in the brain tissue of people who don't have dementia, but the appearance of tangles specifically in the cerebral cortex is associated with the onset of dementia. And tangles are one of two defining characteristics of Alzheimer's disease, the other being beta-amyloid plaques.

Until recently, little was known about neurofibrillary tangles except that they were a result of the abnormal processing of the tau protein. In 1998, however, scientists studying frontotemporal dementia (FTD), an inherited form of neurodegenerative disease, identified a mutation in the tau gene located on chromosome 17. The effect of this mutation in FTD is similar to what happens in Alzheimer's — the twisting of tau protein threads and the accumulation of tangles in the cell.

Furthermore, accumulation of these protein tangles appears to have a more direct effect on neurons than amyloid plaques. The tangles interfere with the transportation of nutrients in cells and the transmission of electric impulses between cells, leading to the collapse of vital cell functions.

It's possible that the production of beta-amyloid may stimulate the formation of tangles, perhaps through upsetting calcium levels within cells. However, the relationship between beta-amyloid and tau tangles remains unclear.

### Inflammatory responses

Various studies have observed profound inflammation in the brains of people with Alzheimer's. Inflammation is your body's response to injury or infection and a natural part of the healing process.

Even as beta-amyloid plaques develop in the space between neurons, immune cells (microglia) are at work getting rid of dead cells and other waste products in the brain. Scientists speculate that the microglia may view plaques as foreign substances in the body and are trying to destroy them, triggering the inflammatory response. Or the microglia may be trying to remove damaged neurons. The microglia may also activate other compounds that cause inflammation. These include the protein interleukin-1, the enzyme COX-2 and a group of proteins, known as complement, which take action against cells marked by microglia for attack. Although researchers believe the inflammation occurs before plaques have fully formed, they aren't sure how this development relates to the disease process. There's also debate about whether inflammation has a damaging effect on neurons or whether it is beneficial in clearing away plaques.

## Oxidative stress

Evidence suggests that beta-amyloid aggregation and possibly the inflammatory response may lead to damage of the mitochondria, the energy factories of the cell. Damaged mitochondria tend to overproduce highly reactive molecules called free radicals. Normally, free radicals perform a number of useful tasks. But too many free radicals cause what is known as oxidative stress. They overwhelm and damage cells, resulting in tissue breakdown and damage to DNA.

## Calcium levels

Studies of beta-amyloid aggregations show that these aggregations may trigger the entry of calcium into neurons in excessive amounts. Calcium, which is usually obtained through your diet, assists in the transmission of impulse messages between cells. But too much calcium in a cell can lead to cell death.

## Other risk factors

Studies of people who developed Alzheimer's disease with no previous family history of dementia indicate that genes aren't the only source of the disease. A number of nongenetic risk factors appear to be associated with Alzheimer's. Some factors, such as age, are definitely established. Others are still under investigation.

**Age.** As discussed in Chapter 1, both the total number of cases of Alzheimer's (prevalence) and the number of new AD cases reported (incidence) rise dramatically with age, doubling every 5 years after the age of 65. Some researchers speculate that Alzheimer's is an inevitable consequence of aging. In other words, if you live long enough you will eventually develop Alzheimer's. However, the fact that many older adults, including people in their 90s or 100s, display sharp memories and intact cognitive skills contradicts this theory.

Other scientists postulate that Alzheimer's occurs within a specific age range and that an increase in the prevalence of AD levels off around the age of 95. A growing consensus is that although Alzheimer's is not a normal part of aging, the effects of aging may strengthen the development of AD.

**Sex.** Studies based on the prevalence of Alzheimer's show that more women have dementia than men. This can be explained, at least in part, by the fact that women generally live longer than men and may even survive longer with dementia. Combined data from a number of European studies spanning the years 1988 to 1996 indicates that women may also have a slightly higher risk of developing dementia, particularly Alzheimer's. Scientists don't know the reason for this distinction, but possibilities might include biological differences. The studies have also been questioned for bias in diagnostic testing or for an unequal distribution of risk factors among males and females.

**Education.** The findings of a project known as the Nun Study support the idea that education may protect someone from developing Alzheimer's disease. The researchers examined autobiographies written by a group of nuns at the time of their entrance into a Milwaukee convent. The average age of these new entrants was 22. The essays were measured for their density of ideas — the average number of ideas per 10 words — and their grammatical complexity. The nuns had also willed their brains to research with the intention of an autopsy being performed when they later died. Surprisingly, the researchers found that 90 percent of the nuns who had a low density of ideas in their autobiographies showed evidence of accumulated neurofibrillary tangles in their brains. Those nuns who had had a high density of ideas at the age of 22 had very few tangles when they died.

The Nun Study received a lot of public attention, and subsequent studies mostly confirm the notion that low levels of education might be a risk factor for later development of Alzheimer's. These studies have their limitations, however. Measures of educational levels can be imprecise. And other factors may confuse or obscure the actual impact of education. All of these theories are speculative, and the mechanisms behind the observations remain unknown. Furthermore, although many of the studies are suggestive of education being protective, the findings aren't conclusive.

**Head injury.** The observation that some ex-boxers eventually develop dementia leads to the question of whether serious traumatic injury to the head (for example, with a prolonged loss of consciousness) may be a risk factor for Alzheimer's. Several studies indicate a significant link between the two, especially for men. Other studies find only a slight, nonsignificant correlation between head trauma and Alzheimer's. The debate is still ongoing, but one of the theories is that head injury may interact with APOE ε4, leading to a higher risk of Alzheimer's.

**Risk factors under investigation.** A number of studies suggest a positive correlation between Alzheimer's, high blood pressure and high cholesterol. Depression also has been identified as a possible risk factor for AD. These studies are still in the early phases of research, and scientists are continuing to pursue conclusive evidence in these areas.

Investigators have also looked at smoking and exposure to occupational hazards such as glues, pesticides, fertilizers or, even, electromagnetic fields as potential contributors to Alzheimer's. Smoking was at one point thought to be protective, but this hypothesis is contradicted in later studies. Aluminum, which has sometimes been found in the brains of people with Alzheimer's, has been a matter of debate for years. Results from all of these investigations have been inconsistent, and at this point, there's still no irrefutable evidence regarding any environmental or lifestyle factor increasing a person's risk of Alzheimer's.

## A complicated process

The emerging picture of Alzheimer's involves an intricate disease process that may include all of the elements described above — genetic susceptibility, beta-amyloid aggregation, neurofibrillary tangles, inflammation, oxidative stress, cellular imbalance and as yet unknown risk factors. And the difficulty of predicting who will develop Alzheimer's may remain a characteristic of the disease in and of itself. Although researchers may identify common physiological pathways for Alzheimer's in most people, its occurrence in each person may be precipitated by a different combination of genetic and environmental triggers.

Although key elements of Alzheimer's disease are being revealed, many important questions about these elements remain unanswered. What roles do plaques and tangles play in the injury and eventual death of neurons? What part does inflammation play? What environmental factors, if any, affect the onset and progression of the disease? Will treatment targeted at eliminating plaques and tangles also address the mental and physical manifestations of AD? What is it that allows some people in their 90s or 100s to retain their memory and intellectual skills? These are some of the issues scientists continue to pursue in the quest to find the cause of Alzheimer's disease.

## What about genetic screening for Alzheimer's?

Although genetic screening kits are available for presenilin 1 (PS1) mutations and for the apolipoprotein E (APOE) allele ε4, most Alzheimer's specialists don't routinely recommend these tests. However, if one person has early-onset Alzheimer's and another close family member is exhibiting signs or symptoms of dementia, screening tests for a PS1 mutation may be useful in making an accurate diagnosis for the second family member.

Most researchers agree that screening for the APOE ε4 gene has little predictive value. In other words, having this gene doesn't mean you will get Alzheimer's, and not having it doesn't mean you won't get Alzheimer's. If preventive treatment becomes available, this test will be more useful to a wider number of people.

# Chapter 5

# Diagnosing Alzheimer's disease

You may feel embarrassed because you constantly forget the names of people you know and the appointments you meant to keep. You may wonder why you feel so anxious or frustrated at the slightest change in your daily routine. You think, perhaps, these symptoms are due to stress or fatigue or getting old. Or you worry that they're the result of disease or even some kind of personal failing. In any case, if you're aware of memory problems or uncharacteristic mood swings, consider consulting a doctor.

Understandably, this can be a difficult step to take. That's because scheduling an appointment with the doctor means admitting there might be a problem with a part of you that you've always depended on. You've counted on your memory — your ability to recall — for accomplishing many tasks and establishing a context for your life experiences. Taking the step, however, is worth the effort. The doctor may be able to identify the cause of your concerns.

If there is a memory problem, then what? The cause may be reversible. And if it's not, a diagnosis may allow you to be treated in a way that helps you manage the condition and take positive steps toward adapting to the new circumstances.

## The importance of an early diagnosis

When memory loss or mood changes are involved, the doctor may consider Alzheimer's disease (AD) as a potential cause. But a diagnosis of Alzheimer's is a process of elimination. The doctor will test for all other possible causes of the signs and symptoms and rule out each cause one by one until the only possibility remaining is Alzheimer's disease.

Why is testing done this way? It's because researchers haven't been able to come up with a definitive test that shows a person has the disease. Researchers haven't yet found biologic or physiologic changes in the body, known as markers, that identify the onset of Alzheimer's with certainty. So a diagnosis of AD is achieved by eliminating all other possibilities. Following this method, doctors are able to make an accurate diagnosis about 90 percent of the time. A diagnosis with 100 percent certainty can only be accomplished by doing an autopsy, when brain tissue can be examined directly under a microscope.

OK, you may be thinking to yourself, since there is no completely accurate diagnosis for this progressive and incurable disease, why is there a need to make a diagnosis at all? For one thing, another condition may be causing the problem, and if this condition can be identified, it may be treated. It's estimated that 5 percent to 10 percent of people showing memory loss, confusion and other signs of dementia have a potentially reversible illness, such as metabolic problems, depression, drug intoxication, thyroid problems or vitamin deficiencies. The earlier the diagnosis, generally the easier it is to treat one of these conditions.

If testing indicates that a dementia such as Alzheimer's is present, an early diagnosis is important for several reasons:
- Although no drug exists that can stop or reverse Alzheimer's, drugs do exist that, if administered early enough, may help treat the symptoms of early-stage Alzheimer's and improve the person's quality of life. Whether these drugs might possibly slow the progress of the disease is being researched.
- Treatment of a concurrent condition that may contribute to the dementia, such as depression, anxiety or any one of several

sleep disorders, often results in improved general health and potentially improved cognition.

- Many important legal and financial decisions as well as decisions about medical care need to be made regarding the person and his or her family. An early diagnosis may allow this person to actively participate in these decisions.
- Early diagnosis gives the person time to prepare mentally and emotionally for the changes ahead. Time allows the person to learn more about the disease, which can lessen some of the anxieties and fears. It also allows his or her family to plan adequately for living arrangements and day-to-day care.

## Warning signs of Alzheimer's disease

The 10 warnings signs generally associated with Alzheimer's include:

1. Memory loss
2. Difficulty performing familiar tasks
3. Problems with language
4. Disorientation with regard to time and place
5. Poor or decreased judgment
6. Problems with abstract thinking
7. Misplacing things
8. Changes in mood or behavior
9. Changes in personality
10. Loss of initiative

Adapted from the Alzheimer's Association, 2001.

A person may not experience all of these signs and symptoms. And this list doesn't reflect the order in which signs and symptoms may occur. Nevertheless, the first warning sign of Alzheimer's disease is often forgetfulness. Misplacing the car keys on the same day that he or she also forgots a lunch date doesn't necessarily mean the person has Alzheimer's. Forgetfulness must persist for months and progressively worsen. Usually another symptom or two will accompany the memory loss.

## How does the doctor know if it's Alzheimer's disease?

Although no single test can be used to diagnose Alzheimer's disease, specialists can accurately identify the disease 9 times out of 10 by using a combination of tests and evaluations. The criteria most often used to diagnose Alzheimer's are established by the American Psychiatric Association and can be found in a medical handbook called the *Diagnostic and Statistical Manual of Mental Disorders*, Fourth Edition (referred to as DSM-IV). For a diagnosis of Alzheimer's, according to DSM-IV, these criteria must be met:

1. The person has multiple — at least two — problems with cognition. One of these problems must be memory loss, as evidenced by a failure to recognize or recall the names of objects despite being able to see, hear or touch them. Besides memory loss, these problems include one or more of the following:

- Difficulty with speaking or following conversations
- Inability to perform complex coordinated physical movements
- Difficulty with visuospatial tasks such as staying oriented as you move through your house or drawing geometric designs
- Problems with planning, organizing, sequencing or thinking abstractly

2. Of the cognitive problems the person has, each problem causes significant impairment in work life and social life and represents a decline from his or her former abilities.

3. The signs and symptoms have come on gradually and are steadily getting worse.

4. Medical evaluation has determined that the cognitive problems aren't due to other conditions such as a brain tumor, a stroke or an infection.

5. The cognitive problems don't occur exclusively during a period of delirium.

6. The signs and symptoms aren't better accounted for by a condition such as depression or other disorders that affect emotional balance.

## The challenge of making a diagnosis

There is a wide range in the estimated number of people with Alzheimer's disease — between 2 million and 4 million people. That's because scientists are discovering that some of the symptoms of the disease may occur earlier than previously thought. In other words, the exact point at which Alzheimer's may be said to be present in the body is becoming more and more difficult to determine. Definitions of mild Alzheimer's vary, and different doctors may use different criteria. Furthermore, diagnosis of AD is generally obtained by excluding all other conditions that might be causing the signs and symptoms. As a result of all these reasons, it often becomes a challenge to determine precisely who has Alzheimer's and who doesn't. Many scientists and medical professionals worldwide are working to come up with improved criteria for a diagnosis.

## How is the medical evaluation done?

Although a doctor may be the primary contact, a whole team of medical professionals may be involved in an evaluation, including nurses, social workers and perhaps a few specialists, such as a psychiatrist or neurologist. The evaluation may include a medical history, a physical and neurological examination, a mental status assessment, and psychiatric and neuropsychologic assessments. Some of these tests are used to identify or eliminate other diseases or types of dementia. Other tests are used to assess the person's level of cognitive functioning.

### Medical history

To compile a medical history, the doctor will probably interview the person and someone he or she lives with or is in regular contact with. The purpose of the interview is to identify the signs and symptoms and create a chronology of events. The doctor will want to assess any changes in the way the person performs tasks in comparison with a previous level of performance, including doing household activities, handling finances or interacting socially. He or she will also record any personality changes. Because it's difficult to be objective or remember every detail, it's important to involve others in the evaluation. This allows the doctor to hear another perspective.

The doctor may ask the person and a spouse, family member or friend the following questions:

- What is the daily routine like?
- When were the first symptoms noticed?
- Have the symptoms grown worse over time or remained constant?
- Are the symptoms interfering with daily activities?

The doctor may also ask questions about any past or ongoing medical problems, a family history of dementia and other diseases, the social and cultural background of the family and any over-the-counter or prescription medications the person may take.

### Physical and neurologic examination

Assessing the person's current health status is a crucial step in the evaluation. Any number of physical factors may have an impact on cognitive functions. The examination may include:

- A physical exam to identify medical illnesses that may contribute to cognitive impairment, such as congestive heart failure or hypothyroidism.
- A neurologic exam to identify signs of Parkinson's disease, strokes, tumors or other medical conditions that may impair memory and thinking as well as physical function.
- Brain imaging — computerized tomography (CT) or magnetic resonance imaging (MRI) — to detect strokes, tumors, hydrocephalus or other structural abnormalities. In Alzheimer's, there may be shrinkage (atrophy) in the structures of the brain, such as the hippocampus, that are associated with memory.
- Blood and urine tests to pinpoint thyroid problems, anemia, medication levels, infections and other factors.
- An electrocardiogram — a record of electric impulses as the heart pumps blood — and possibly a chest X-ray to measure cardiovascular health and check for factors that may influence vascular dementia.

# Imaging technology for a look inside your body

To make an accurate diagnosis of Alzheimer's, a doctor may be assisted by highly sophisticated technology that produces clear pictures of the internal organs.

**Computerized tomography.** Computerized tomography, also known as a CT scan, is an imaging technique that's used extensively to examine the brain and other organs. An X-ray beam passing through the body generates the image. But a CT scan provides more information than an ordinary X-ray. That's because part of the X-ray machine is rapidly rotated around the body so that images are obtained from all angles. A computer processes these images and combines them into a single, detailed, cross-sectional scan.

**Magnetic resonance imaging.** Rather than using X-rays to produce an image, magnetic resonance imaging (MRI) uses magnetic fields and radio waves. The machine detects small energy signals emitted by the atoms that make up body tissues and constructs images

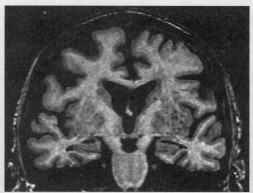

An MRI of the brain

based on that information. The pictures produced with MRI are similar to those taken with CT, but they're more detailed and may show slightly different tissues.

**Positron emission tomography.** Positron emission tomography (PET) is a fairly new and expensive imaging technique that detects emissions from a small amount of radioactive material that's injected into the body. Two different detectors placed on opposite sides of the body detect the emissions. This technique has the advantage of being able to reveal the way in which tissue actually uses energy (see pages C4 and C5 in the color section). PET isn't routinely used in diagnosing Alzheimer's although an occasional need for it exists in some clinical-related or research-related cases.

- An assessment of the person's nutritional status and body mass index (BMI). The BMI is a formula that is determined by both weight and height. It's a better estimate of body fat and health risks than the number on a bathroom scale.

### Mental status assessment

To determine which cognitive functions may be affected and how severely, a clinician will assess the person's mental status. The assessment may include interviews and written tests to evaluate:
- Sense of time and place
- Ability to understand, speak and remember
- Ability to perform daily activities, such as paying bills and operating home appliances

Additional tests of mental status may include doing simple calculations, spelling a word backward and drawing a simple design.

### Psychiatric and neuropsychologic assessments

A psychiatric assessment can help determine if the person is depressed or has a condition that may mimic dementia or accompany Alzheimer's. The assessment may also help identify patterns in cognitive functions that are clues to the underlying condition.

Neuropsychologic tests are designed to evaluate memory, ability to reason, problem-solving ability, language competency and coordination between vision and muscular movement. These tests may be critical for differentiating between depression and dementia, especially in the early stages of Alzheimer's. The test profiles can also help differentiate Alzheimer's from conditions such as Lewy body dementia and frontotemporal dementia.

## Understanding the results of an evaluation

At the end of the evaluation, the doctor may designate the person's condition as one of the following:
- **Possible Alzheimer's.** The doctor believes Alzheimer's disease is the primary cause of the signs and symptoms but suspects that another disorder is affecting its progression and obscuring the disease process.

- **Probable Alzheimer's.** The doctor has ruled out other disorders and concluded that the signs and symptoms are most likely caused by Alzheimer's disease.
- **Some other form of dementia.** The doctor believes some other disorder such as vascular dementia, frontotemporal dementia or Lewy body dementia, and not Alzheimer's, is the cause of the signs and symptoms.

## What autopsy reveals

A diagnosis of Alzheimer's disease with 100 percent accuracy requires an examination of brain tissue. This is typically done with an autopsy after a person dies. An autopsy of a person with Alzheimer's usually reveals the characteristic plaques and tangles in the brain (see the sidebar "Plaques and tangles" on page 30). This information is important for research purposes. However, it should be understood that a diagnosis of probable Alzheimer's is very accurate, even without an autopsy.

## What happens after diagnosis?

A diagnosis of Alzheimer's disease can be frightening and difficult to deal with. You or a family member who's just received a diagnosis may experience a range of emotions, including disbelief and denial, anger, sadness and even acceptance. You'll need to give yourself time to work through these feelings and adjust emotionally. Remember that you're not alone. Millions of people in the United States and around the world have Alzheimer's. They're coming to terms with the disease, just as you or a family member is.

Don't be afraid to ask others for help. Family and friends can provide ready assistance when you need it. A doctor, nurse or psychologist also can help you and your family cope with this time of change. A medical professional can work with you to develop a strategy to handle the disease as it progresses. He or she can help you determine the right time and the manner in which to tell others of the diagnosis. There also may be resources in your community that can provide valuable advice and assistance, including local chapters of the Alzheimer's Association or Area Agency on Aging.

As mentioned before, one of the benefits of an early diagnosis is that it gives you and your family time to learn about and anticipate changes that may accompany the disease. A person may still be in a good position to make his or her own health care and financial decisions or authorize others to do so when the need arises. In addition, early diagnosis gives a family time to modify the home environment and daily routine to accommodate the person's evolving needs. More information about the preparatory steps you or a family member may take can be found on page 161 of this book.

## Alzheimer's legacy

Alzheimer's disease makes no distinction between the famous and not so famous, the accomplished artist and the average citizen. Winston Churchill (prime minister), Rita Hayworth (actress), Ralph Waldo Emerson (poet), Sugar Ray Robinson (world champion boxer) and Aaron Copland (composer) all achieved great success in their respective fields. Yet their success could not protect these celebrities from the debilitating effects of Alzheimer's. Millions of people today, including former President Ronald Reagan, live with this illness.

# Part 3

*Treating Alzheimer's disease*

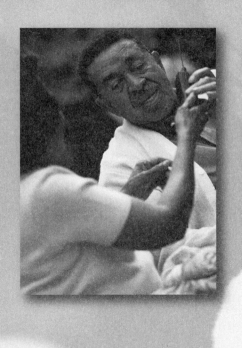

# Chapter 6

# Treating the symptoms of Alzheimer's disease

Although researchers are working to develop therapies that can halt or delay the progression of Alzheimer's disease, and possibly even prevent it, no such therapy is available yet. Current treatment is focused on managing the cognitive and behavioral symptoms of the disease and thereby improving the quality of life for people with Alzheimer's. This means treatment aims to, for example, improve memory, calm anxieties and help people with dementia to remain alert in waking hours or sleep well at night.

Treatment is most often a combination of drug therapies and personal care. Drug therapies range from medications developed specifically for treating the cognitive symptoms of Alzheimer's to drugs used broadly in the mental health field, such as antidepressants and antipsychotics. Personal care is administered in a number of ways and a variety of situations.

## Working toward treatment goals

Living with a disease such as Alzheimer's can be a challenge that stretches the courage, fortitude, patience, flexibility, creativity and adaptive skills of everyone involved. It requires trust and honesty in dealing with complex personal issues. As the disease progresses, the types and combinations of treatments will change. What worked in the mild stage of Alzheimer's may no longer be appropriate for the moderate or severe stage.

In recognizing that Alzheimer's disease presents a difficult challenge, recognize also that you don't have to face this challenge alone. More and more, experts and health care professionals understand and emphasize the need for team effort — a team that includes the caregiver, doctors, nurses, social workers, clinicians, friends, family and, most importantly, the person with Alzheimer's. One of the benefits of the increasing national focus on Alzheimer's disease is the growing number of resources available to people with the condition and to their caregivers. What you need to do is find out how to take advantage of those resources.

If you or someone you know has received a diagnosis of Alzheimer's, here are three key things to remember:

### Know your resources

In order to make use of the resources available to you, you have to know where to find them. The Alzheimer's Association is a key source of information and may be able to refer you to specific resources in your community. With local chapters throughout the United States, this organization can help you find medical specialists and financial planners, support groups, in-home services such as Meals-On-Wheels, respite care and assisted-living and nursing home facilities. At the back of this book, you'll find a list of organizations, including the Alzheimer's Association, for people with Alzheimer's, their families and their caregivers.

### Ask for help

Many people dealing with Alzheimer's, whether it be the person with the disease or the caregiver, find it difficult to ask for help. They often feel that because they're adults, they should be able to handle the pressures and stress on their own. This mind-set all too frequently makes the problems worse.

For the person with early-stage Alzheimer's, it can be frightening to admit to yourself that you have the disease, which might certainly make you reluctant to seek help. But at a time when you're coming to terms with the disease, it's important to remain connected to your family and friends. Where you falter, they can help.

If you're the caregiver, wearing yourself out to the point of exhaustion is not beneficial to you or your loved one. To provide care for others, you also need to care for yourself, both physically and emotionally. This can come about by enlisting the help of family members and friends, obtaining advice from experts and thoughtfully addressing the problems at hand.

**Don't give up**

Although Alzheimer's disease will bring dramatic changes to your life, remember that there will continue to be good moments and bad moments and even, very likely, humorous moments. So, when possible, step back from the immediate demands of living and focus your mind on something else. Enjoy a morning cup of coffee or watch a favorite movie. Though it may be a tired cliche, it's still good advice — sometimes you just have to have room to breathe.

These three fundamental steps can help you actively participate with your doctor and a health care team to achieve your treatment goals. Access to a full arsenal of therapies may put the manageable aspects of the disease, for a time at least, under your control. And applying what you've learned about Alzheimer's, it is hoped, will assist you or a loved one in facing the challenges of the disease with dignity and grace.

## Treating cognitive symptoms

As discussed earlier, one of the main neurotransmitters affected by Alzheimer's disease is acetylcholine. Scientists know that levels of acetylcholine drop sharply in people with Alzheimer's, a drop at least partly caused by an enzyme known as acetylcholinesterase. So scientists have been focusing on developing drugs to keep, or inhibit, the acetylcholinesterase from acting on the acetylcholine. All of the drugs currently approved by the Food and Drug Administration (FDA) for treating the cognitive impairment caused by Alzheimer's work in this manner. Thus, the drugs as a group are called cholinesterase (ko-lin-ES-tur-ays) inhibitors.

Currently, cholinesterase inhibitors are used only in the mild to moderate stages of Alzheimer's — generally 3 to 6 years after diagnosis. During this time, these inhibitors play a valuable role in the management of the disease. They not only stabilize cognitive function but also seem to have a positive effect on behavior.

Some scientists think it's possible that cholinesterase inhibitors exert a protective effect on neurons. Therefore, these scientists wonder if taking such a drug in the earliest stage of Alzheimer's may also be helpful. Beyond the moderate stage, the drugs appear to be ineffective and the cognitive decline resumes. The long-term effects of these medications aren't known, but studies are under way to observe them.

---

### Acetylcholine: The thoughtful messenger

Acetylcholine is one of the principal chemical messengers within your body, occurring in both your central and peripheral nervous systems. It controls muscle contractions and hormone secretion and also plays a key role, if still not completely understood, in thinking and memory skills.

In the 1970s, neuroscientists became aware of the dramatic drop in the level of acetylcholine in the brains of people with Alzheimer's. Since then, much research has been focused on this neurotransmitter. Researchers have learned that the acetylcholine deficit is related directly to the severity of dementia. This evidence has inspired therapies designed to alter the levels of acetylcholine in the brain in hopes that this action would improve the symptoms of Alzheimer's.

Although scientists are still not sure of the exact role acetylcholine plays in thinking and memory, most agree that it's involved in what is called selective attention. This term refers to the way your brain filters incoming information and processes some messages while ignoring others. Some researchers speculate that a shortage of acetylcholine may have a tremendous impact on conscious awareness as well as on memory information and retrieval.

## Types of cholinesterase inhibitors

The currently available cholinesterase inhibitors are donepezil, rivastigmine and galantamine. Although these medications are generally well tolerated, gastrointestinal problems are common side effects. These include nausea, diarrhea, stomach pain, loss of appetite and vomiting.

**Donepezil (Aricept).** Approved by the FDA in 1996, donepezil is the most commonly prescribed cholinesterase inhibitor. It comes in tablet form and is taken orally once a day. The doctor may start someone with a dose of 5 milligrams (mg) and then increase the dose to 10 mg if the person tolerates the drug well. In clinical trials, people with Alzheimer's who took donepezil did better on memory and reasoning assessments than did those who were given an inactive substance (placebo). One of the benefits of donepezil is that its side effects are generally mild.

**Rivastigmine (Exelon).** This drug is similar to donepezil in its action. Rivastigmine, however, is taken orally twice a day and comes in capsule or liquid form. Dosages can range from 6 mg to 12 mg a day. Higher doses of rivastigmine have been shown to be more effective than lower doses but also cause more severe side effects. If your doctor prescribes this drug, the person will probably start out at a low dose — to minimize discomfort — but the dose may be increased gradually over time. Taking the medication with food may help as well.

**Galantamine (Reminyl).** Galantamine is the newest cholinesterase inhibitor on the market. It improves both cognition and behavior. Its long-term effects have not yet been observed, but it was well tolerated during clinical trials. Galantamine comes in tablet form, and the dosage is increased gradually, generally to no more than 12 mg twice a day. Its side effects are usually mild, similar to those of donepezil.

People who are taking a cholinesterase inhibitor often wonder if the medication is doing any good. It may be tempting to stop taking the medication if they don't see any apparent benefits. But remember that these drugs are designed to maintain cognitive functions, and people who abruptly stop taking the medication often experience a dramatic drop in these functions.

Aside from medications, using memory aids also can help the person supplement cognitive losses and maintain a degree of independence and dignity. Write down information regarding appointments and social events and keep it in visible places, along with clocks and calendars. Create a list of the day's activities, including specific instructions for tasks such as getting dressed and preparing food. Make a list of important phone numbers. Label drawers with their respective contents and label entrances to different rooms with their functions, for example, "bathroom" and "bedroom."

For a caregiver, as the disease process progresses, it may be more important to provide reassurance rather than orient the person to the current time or place or the real version of events. If the person becomes worried about a loved one who is no longer living, for example, it's often more comforting to reassure him or her that everything is OK than to insist upon a recognition of reality.

## Treating behavioral symptoms

As Alzheimer's disease progresses, alterations in mood and behavior become common. This may result in part from damage to neurotransmitters and the impairment of cell communication. It may also be a result of damage to the limbic system — the part of your brain associated with emotions. Many abnormal behaviors, however, are an outgrowth of the progressive inability to remember things, reason with others and solve problems. Difficult behaviors often associated with Alzheimer's include:

- Aggression
- Agitation
- Delusions
- Hallucinations
- Resisting help
- Suspiciousness or paranoia
- Sleep disturbances
- Wandering

These behaviors are discussed in the Quick Guide.

These behaviors may be the only way the person with Alzheimer's can express discomfort, stress and frustration. It's important to remember that someone with Alzheimer's is gradually losing his or her language skills. Even if speech remains intact, the person may have difficulty forming and expressing thoughts correctly. The behaviors may be a means to communicate feelings and needs.

Without giving it much thought, it's easy to label a challenging behavior, or even the person with Alzheimer's, as bad or a problem. But it's important to resist labeling for two major reasons. For one thing, troublesome behaviors are rarely acted out on purpose or manipulatively. They arise from the disease process. For another thing, these labels create the expectation of good behavior — an expectation that the person with Alzheimer's may not be able to meet. This can foster a sense of futility or resignation in the person you're caring for.

### Secondary causes

Many times behavioral problems occur not because of cognitive impairment but because of other issues. Health, psychological, environmental and social factors all can affect a person with Alzheimer's disease. Problems stemming from these factors are termed excess disability. That means the problems occur in addition to the signs and symptoms caused directly by Alzheimer's. If these added problems are identified, a caregiver can focus on eliminating, modifying or preventing the aggravating factors. Therefore, when addressing behavioral issues, it's helpful to think about other factors that may be contributors.

**Health problems.** An underlying physical problem can elicit complaints from just about anyone. Someone with Alzheimer's is no exception, but because the person may have difficulty communicating what's wrong, he or she may exhibit behavioral problems. Difficult behavior can arise from pain, hunger, fatigue, medication side effects, dehydration, constipation or a physical illness such as an infection or a respiratory condition. Impaired hearing or vision can further isolate a person and be a frequent source of hallucinations and delusions. Distinguishing between symptoms caused by Alzheimer's or caused by a different source can be challenging.

Possible indications that there's a secondary cause include a challenging behavior that's new, a sudden decline in function or a worsening of confusion. If any of these situations occur, you may need to consult your doctor. Treatment of a secondary problem often results in improved behavior and cognition, even though the improvement may be temporary.

**Psychological issues.** Anxiety and depression are common among people with Alzheimer's. Anxiety is often expressed by showing excessive concern over upcoming events or by wandering, screaming or acting aggressively. Feelings of anxiety can be caused by a number of factors, including illness, abuse, loss of a loved one

## The ABC method

Heading off problems before they occur can be an effective way for a caregiver to manage behavior. This is sometimes called the ABC method, where A stands for antecedent, B for behavior and C for consequence. Most behaviors have a cause or antecedent. And behaviors generally lead to consequences.

As a caregiver, you may be tempted to concentrate mainly on the consequences of the behavior because these often demand immediate attention. But a little forethought can go a long way. By addressing antecedents first, you may be able to avert both the behavior and the consequences. For example, seeing a car in the driveway may cause a person with Alzheimer's to have outbursts of anger because the person may be reminded that he or she can no longer drive. Attempts to soothe the person may require a tremendous amount of time and energy. Using the ABC approach, you might decide to keep the car parked out of sight. This addresses the antecedent of the outburst and eliminates needless frustration and wasted energy.

Not all behaviors have antecedents all of the time. But whether a behavior has an antecedent or not, being adaptive is an important part of caregiving. In some cases, such as wandering, you may wish to simply go along with the behavior. If the behavior is relatively benign and can be done in a safe place, such as pacing in an enclosed yard or an open room, it may be an appropriate outlet for feelings that might otherwise be expressed in a more threatening manner. Try to be creative. See what works and what doesn't. And go easy on yourself. If an approach isn't successful one day, keep in mind that you're doing your best. Simply try something else the next day.

or cognitive decline. Feelings of depression may translate into tear-fulness, thoughts of worthlessness and concerns about being a burden. Depression may also come across as a worsening of thinking and reasoning skills, and result in social withdrawal, weight loss, disruptive behavior and decreased functional abilities.

Fortunately, both anxiety and depression are treatable (see page 37). Obtaining a diagnosis from the doctor can lead to more realistic expectations for the caregiver and better knowledge of how to communicate with and care for the person with Alzheimer's.

Support groups and professional counseling may help people in the early stages of Alzheimer's who are depressed but still communicating well. Physical exercise and planned activities also can help alleviate symptoms of anxiety or depression by providing a sense of purpose, self-worth and accomplishment.

It's also important for the person with Alzheimer's to avoid caffeine and alcohol, as these can be stimulants. If symptoms of anxiety and depression are severe, treatment may include anti-anxiety (anxiolytic) or antidepressant medications.

**Environmental factors.** Understimulation or overstimulation brought on by your surroundings can have a significant impact on behavior. With nothing to do, a person with Alzheimer's may become bored or restless and resort to wandering or yelling to release these feelings. On the other hand, multiple or unnecessary stimuli may confuse and overwhelm the person. Television shows may be misunderstood or mistaken for reality, resulting in frightened or angry reactions. Disembodied voices coming from radios, overhead paging systems or people out of sight also can contribute to confusion, paranoia, agitation, and even hallucinations and delusions. Creating a safe, serene and predictable environment can provide a sense of familiarity and comfort to the person with Alzheimer's and reduce disruptive behavior.

**Social factors.** Although a person with Alzheimer's experiences a progressive loss of ability to communicate with others, he or she will still retain basic human needs to belong, to be loved and to feel useful. Social isolation can lead to depression and anxiety as well as to any number of unwanted behaviors, including agitation, delusions, aggression and wandering.

One way to circumvent these types of problems and improve quality of life is to make sure the person with Alzheimer's stays involved in daily activities and chores. At the same time, it's important to involve the person at a level that he or she can feel comfortable of achieving success. What a person with Alzheimer's is able to do may vary from day to day. Sometimes everyday tasks, such as getting dressed, may seem overwhelming. Try to break the task into steps, limit choices and allow extra time for the person to accomplish the chore. Rushing the process or pressuring the person to remember by using reason, argument or accusation may only cause panic. More details on how to assist a loved one in everyday tasks can be found in the Quick Guide.

A 1999 study funded by the National Institute of Nursing Research revealed that allowing people with Alzheimer's to accomplish as much on their own as possible reinforced their existing skills and helped maintain their independence. Even though the time needed to finish dressing on their own nearly doubled, disruptive behaviors decreased and appropriate requests for help increased.

Planning more recreational types of activities also can help relieve behavioral symptoms. Enjoyable pastimes may include singing, painting, playing board games, walking or reading. The activity is not so important as the level of fulfillment and social interaction that can be derived from doing it. After all, holding a newspaper at a proper angle to read is certainly not as vital as the happiness the person may derive from actually trying to read it.

## Medication therapies for behavioral symptoms

Sometimes personal care and interactions aren't enough to soothe challenging behavior or alleviate the symptoms of depression or anxiety. In these cases, your doctor may prescribe certain drugs that can help improve behavioral symptoms. Although medications such as the following may be of some benefit, they're often used as a second line of defense in Alzheimer's. That's because these drugs can intensify cognitive losses, and their side effects are generally more pronounced in older adults.

**Antipsychotics.** Medications called antipsychotics or neuroleptics may be used to treat aggression, delusions and hallucinations. Antipsychotics are divided into two major groups: conventional and atypical. Both groups work by blocking certain neurotransmitter receptors, particularly dopamine, in the hopes of regulating emotions. Atypical antipsychotics also act on serotonin, which may be a reason why these medications generally have fewer side effects than conventional antipsychotics. The side effects include muscle spasms, rigidity, tremor and gait disturbance. Antipsychotics also block acetylcholine receptors, which are already in short supply in a person with Alzheimer's. This action tends to accelerate cognitive decline. Commonly prescribed antipsychotic drugs include:

- Olanzapine (Zyprexa): Atypical antipsychotic used to treat delusions and hallucinations with associated agitation, anxiety and insomnia
- Quetiapine (Seroquel): Atypical antipsychotic used to treat psychotic symptoms, agitation and insomnia. It is less potent than olanzapine but with fewer side effects
- Haloperidol (Haldol): Conventional antipsychotic used to treat delusions and hallucinations. Unfortunately, usage brings a high risk of muscle rigidity and tremor
- Risperidone (Risperdal): Atypical antipsychotic that, if used at a dosage of less than 6 mg a day, has few side effects. A higher dosage may cause side effects such as rigidity and tremor

**Anxiolytics.** Symptoms of anxiety may be relieved with anxiolytic (ang-zee-oe-LIT-ik) agents known, as a group, as benzodiazepines. These medications work efficiently in the short term, but their benefits gradually decrease with prolonged use. Some anxiolytics take a few weeks to begin working, which also may limit their use. Side effects include sleepiness, decreased learning and memory, dizziness and loss of coordination, and possibly even more agitation. Recommended anxiolytics include:

- Lorazepam (Ativan)
- Oxazepam (Serax)
- Buspirone (Buspar)
- Zolpidem (Ambien)

One major advance in psychopharmacology is that newer drugs are replacing benzodiazepines as the treatment of choice for anxiety. A group of antidepressants known as SSRIs are now frequently prescribed for anxiety. It takes about 4 weeks to see their therapeutic effect. SSRIs are described in the section below.

**Antidepressants.** If a person with Alzheimer's receives a diagnosis of major depression, drug therapy is often recommended. Tricyclic antidepressants, such as nortriptyline (Pamelor) and desipramine (Norpramin), were often prescribed but they're rarely used anymore because they may inhibit acetylcholine transmission along with causing other side effects. A more recently developed group of antidepressants called selective serotonin reuptake inhibitors (SSRIs) have proved to be effective in people with Alzheimer's while causing relatively few side effects. SSRIs act primarily by blocking serotonin receptors in the brain, yet leaving acetylcholine receptors undisturbed. Common side effects of certain SSRIs are anxiety and agitation, and so they should be used with caution in people who already exhibit these symptoms. Other side effects include insomnia, tremor, nausea, diarrhea, headache, decreased appetite, dizziness, sweating and dry mouth. These side effects may go away on their own. Side effects may also be minimized by starting the medications at half the recommended dose but gradually increasing to a standard dose over a period of one or two weeks.

Commonly prescribed antidepressants include:

- Fluoxetine (Prozac)
- Sertraline (Zoloft)
- Paroxetine (Paxil)
- Citalopram (Celexa)

## A good perspective

The distinction between an incurable disease and an untreatable one should be noted as you contemplate the options of Alzheimer's treatment. Alzheimer's is still incurable, but it's also a treatable disease through the use of medications and personal care. Even as the symptoms of Alzheimer's progressively worsen, therapies to improve cognition and ease challenging behaviors greatly enhance the quality of life for people with Alzheimer's and for caregivers. A personal focus remains the strongest weapon against this unrelenting disease. The intensive research for a way to halt or delay Alzheimer's is the subject of the next chapter.

# Chapter 7

# New directions
# in Alzheimer's treatment

A s Alzheimer's research continues to move forward, some scientists feel that they may be reaching the "beginning of the end" in terms of finding a means to fight the disease. Understanding the disease process is one of the major areas of research today. Knowing the hows and whys of Alzheimer's will enable experts to find better methods of prevention, diagnosis, treatment and care.

In order to test new ideas, researchers must submit their theories to rigorous clinical trials. Clinical trials are used to evaluate a potential treatment on humans that has previously shown effectiveness against disease, either in a test-tube environment or in limited studies on animals. The treatment becomes established and generally accepted only after it has passed the trial process, which typically lasts several years.

The overriding goals of clinical trials are to test if the treatment works and to make sure it's safe. Researchers carefully design the trial procedures so that they can learn as much as possible while minimizing the risk of injury to participants. The researchers must try to determine if the benefits are actually a result of treatment, rather than chance or other factors.

## The clinical trial process

New drug treatments are tested in five stages, which occur in sequence. Testing at any of these stages may be done at multiple sites. Researchers may stop the trial at any point due to adverse side effects or other concerns.

**Preclinical phase.** At this stage, the tests are performed on animals or in medical laboratories. Preclinical trials help researchers identify treatments that are unsafe or ineffective. If a treatment doesn't work in the lab, researchers will not test it on humans.

**Phase I.** This stage is often the first attempt at testing on humans. Researchers try to resolve such questions as:

- What is the correct dosage of the drug?
- How does the human body react to the treatment?
- How long does the treatment work?
- What is the best way to administer the treatment?
- How much of the drug can be administered safely?
- Does the treatment cause harmful side effects?

Between 20 and 80 volunteers usually participate in this phase. Because this may be the first time the drug will be tested on people, no one knows what the risks to the participants will be. So those chosen to participate are often people who would otherwise not be helped by existing therapies for treating their condition.

**Phase II.** Research in phase II tries to determine whether the new treatment works in the way it's intended. Several hundred people might participate in this stage. Some phase II trials may compare a group of people taking a potential new treatment with another group of people taking a placebo — a pill or liquid that looks like the new treatment but has no active ingredients. The group of participants taking the placebo is called the control group. Investigators monitor all study participants for side effects that may occur with the therapy. Various factors about the treatment remain unknown at this point, and so risks are still present.

**Phase III.** Research may move into a phase III study only after the new treatment shows promise and meets the safety standards of the earlier stages. In phase III, participants often are assigned at random to receive either the experimental treatment or the placebo. This random assignment helps to avoid any bias in the study results. Phase III trials are intended to provide additional information regarding the safety of the potential treatment and to demonstrate whether the experimental group or the control group has a better survival rate or fewer side effects.

These trials are usually much larger than phase I or phase II studies, involving several hundred to several thousand people. Large trials make it easier to estimate what would happen if the new treatment were available to everyone with the condition. At the end of a phase III trial, the Food and Drug Administration (FDA) will evaluate the results and either approve or reject the treatment for general use.

**Phase IV.** This stage monitors the new treatment after the FDA approves it. In a phase IV trial, investigators keep records of reported side effects and any other results that occur in people taking the treatment. A control group is usually not necessary for this phase because the treatment has already been approved. Phase IV trials aren't always required. In some cases, the FDA may ask drug manufacturers to perform the studies to be sure there are no additional side effects or the known side effects are not too serious. Sometimes drug companies launch phase IV studies in the hopes of showing their drug is better than a competitor's product. Companies also use phase IV studies to explore and possibly expand usage of the treatment.

## Research protocols

The multistage clinical trial process follows a specific plan of action called a protocol. The protocol explains the objectives of the study, including who may participate, how the results will be measured and the reasons why a study may be stopped. To ensure the safety of those in the study, the organization that sponsors the study must approve the protocol. In addition, an institutional review board (IRB) at each study site reviews the protocol to be sure participants will be treated safely, humanely and fairly. The IRB also discusses issues such as whether the likely benefits of the treatment outweigh the risks associated with it.

**Informed consent**
Before starting a trial, all participants must sign an informed consent form. This form must explain what will happen during the trial and what are the known risks and benefits of taking part in it. By signing the form, you agree to participate in the trial. However,

## How to participate in a clinical trial

It's difficult, if not impossible, for scientists to conduct research without volunteer participants. This is where the public can play a vital part in the pursuit of better treatment and prevention of diseases such as Alzheimer's. Nevertheless, a decision to enroll in a clinical trial should be considered carefully. In the case of Alzheimer's, this decision often rests with the entire family, rather than just one person. To help families with this decision, the Alzheimer's Association has prepared the following list of considerations:

- Along with your physician, explore whether it's in your loved one's best interest to become involved.
- Be prepared to answer questions about your loved one's condition.
- Expect further screening by the study site to determine eligibility for the trial. Only a minority of interested people may qualify for a particular trial.
- Be aware of the time commitment and other responsibilities involved in participating, such as making trips to the study site, administering the drug and reporting health-related changes to the study coordinators.
- Understand that clinical studies may involve some risk, as they determine the effectiveness and safety of a drug. By the time a drug reaches testing in humans, however, researchers are fairly optimistic of obtaining positive results with few side effects.

even after signing, you still have the right to leave the trial at any point — and without penalty.

A person with dementia may not be able to understand a consent form fully. In many cases, a caregiver may be the appropriate person to sign the consent form, either as a representative of the person's best interest (by proxy) or as directed by the person's previously recorded wishes (advance directive). If the caregiver feels uneasy with the trial at any point, he or she can withdraw the person from the study.

- Know that not all participants are given the treatment being tested. In almost every study, there's a group that receives a placebo, or inactive substance, and a group that receives the experimental treatment. This allows researchers to compare the two groups.
- Realize that individuals receiving the placebo are just as important as those receiving the treatment. Clinical drug trials can't be completed without a control group. If the drug yields positive results, the participants who have been given the placebo may now be given the option of receiving the experimental drug.
- Always remember to ask questions. Researchers should be able to answer your questions satisfactorily. If you feel uncomfortable at any point, you always have the option of not continuing with the study.

To find out more about ongoing clinical trials for Alzheimer's disease, you can look up one of the following Internet addresses:

- Alzheimer's Association: Clinical trials
  *www.alz.org/research/clintrials/*
- National Institute on Aging: Alzheimer's Disease Clinical Trials Database *www.alzheimers.org/trials/basicsearch.html*
- National Institutes of Health: Database of all clinical trials
  *www.clinicaltrials.gov*

## How a treatment is approved

After phases I, II and III have been completed, researchers submit an application to the FDA asking permission to make the experimental treatment available to the public. The FDA assembles a panel of experts to review the research data and make a recommendation. The panel may:

- Recommend that the experimental treatment be approved for marketing as submitted
- Require the sponsor to make specific changes before marketing the treatment
- Not approve the treatment due to major problems

The FDA is not required to do what the panel suggests, but the agency usually follows the panel's recommendation.

## Treatment strategies under investigation

Many investigators are looking not only to delay the progression of Alzheimer's disease but also to prevent its onset. Currently, several strategies for treatment or prevention are under investigation. Most of these strategies expand on the ideas discussed earlier regarding the events that some scientists believe are triggered during the Alzheimer's process. So far, some studies have yielded positive results, others negative.

### Anti-inflammatory agents

In an attempt to reduce the inflammation that occurs in the brains of people with Alzheimer's — and, it is hoped, prevent further degeneration of neurons — researchers are looking at a number of anti-inflammatory agents that might accomplish such an objective. These include:

**Prednisone.** Prednisone belongs to a family of anti-inflammatory medications called corticosteroids. A recent study involving 138 people with Alzheimer's attempted to determine whether low doses of prednisone could slow the rate of cognitive decline. The results were unfortunately negative. Furthermore, the treatment group experienced greater behavioral decline than the placebo group. It's possible that higher doses of prednisone may be more successful, but it's doubtful that prolonged treatment would be tolerated in older adults, especially given the behavioral side effects.

**Nonsteroidal anti-inflammatory drugs (NSAIDs).** In a National Institute on Aging study conducted between 1955 and 1994, researchers identified a link between the use of NSAIDs and a lowered risk of developing Alzheimer's. People in the study who regularly took NSAIDs, including ibuprofen (Advil, Motrin), naproxen sodium (Aleve) and indomethacin (Indocin), had a lower risk of developing Alzheimer's than had those who took acetaminophen (Tylenol) or no painkillers. Other epidemiologic studies have also shown that NSAIDs may play a role in slowing the disease process. However, clinical trials aiming to test the use of such drugs against Alzheimer's have had high dropout rates. This suggests that the side effects associated with long-term use of NSAIDs may be unacceptable to many older adults. Typical side effects include stomach irritation, ulcers and possible kidney problems.

Recent study data suggest that some NSAIDs may actually lower beta-amyloid levels in the brain and retard amyloid plaque development and cell death. Further research may show that the greater role NSAIDs play is to decrease amyloid production rather than to reduce inflammation.

A COX-2 inhibitor is a type of NSAID designed to relieve pain with fewer side effects than a traditional NSAID. The first reported trial that used the COX-2 inhibitors celecoxib (Celebrex) and rofecoxib (Vioxx) produced negative results. In another study, one that is ongoing, rofecoxib is being administered to a group of people with mild cognitive impairment (MCI) to see if it can delay onset of Alzheimer's. A third ongoing trial is comparing the potential preventive effects of a traditional NSAID, a COX-2 inhibitor and a placebo among healthy older individuals.

**Estrogen**

Several epidemiologic studies, including a 1997 report based on data from the Baltimore Longitudinal Study of Aging, indicate that the use of estrogen therapy appears to reduce the risk of developing Alzheimer's by 40 percent to 50 percent. However, the results of the largest and longest trial to date involving estrogen and Alzheimer's, published in 2000, showed no differences between the women who received estrogen replacement therapy (ERT) and those who didn't after 1 year. A smaller trial lasting 16 weeks also showed no benefit in administering estrogen for preventing Alzheimer's.

Because there's still no consensus on whether estrogen may work to lower the risk of Alzheimer's or delay its onset, research continues in various clinical trials. Some studies suggest that it may reduce oxidative stress and inflammation or that it may help to prevent the formation of beta-amyloid. Although ultimately it may prove to not be successful in treating Alzheimer's, it's possible that estrogen may have protective characteristics and thus be more successful if used as a means of preventing the disease. But for the time being, estrogen should probably not be taken for the sole purpose of delaying the onset of Alzheimer's.

### Antioxidants

Based on the theory that oxidative stress contributes to the development of Alzheimer's disease (see page 49), a number of studies have focused on the possibility of using antioxidants as a form of treatment for Alzheimer's. Three popular antioxidants include vitamin E, selegiline and ginkgo.

**Vitamin E and selegiline.** Perhaps the best known antioxidant normally used by your body is vitamin E, also known as alpha-tocopherol. Vitamin E is usually obtained from your diet — from food sources such as vegetable oils, soft margarine, eggs, fish, green leafy vegetables, whole-grain products and dried beans. Research has associated vitamin E intake with a reduced risk of Alzheimer's or cognitive impairment. Selegiline (se-LEJ-uh-leen) is an antioxidant compound used to treat Parkinson's disease.

The only large clinical trial to date, with regard to these antioxidants, published its findings in the April 24, 1997, issue of the *New England Journal of Medicine*. It reported that people with moderate Alzheimer's who were given selegiline or high doses of vitamin E, or a combination of both, experienced a 7-month delay in the progression of the disease. Specifically, a dosage of one or both antioxidants delayed the loss of the ability to perform daily activities, the necessity of moving into a nursing home and the progression to severe dementia . Cognition itself did not improve, however, suggesting that these antioxidants may not work as a treatment for improving symptoms in this stage of the disease.

Other, smaller clinical trials involving just selegiline also fail to show cognitive improvement. Vitamin E is undergoing further study, this time with a group of people with mild cognitive impairment (MCI). The trial is designed to find out if vitamin E can prevent or delay the progression from MCI to Alzheimer's — as noted earlier, people with MCI are at high risk of developing Alzheimer's within 4 years of diagnosis.

Although vitamin E doesn't require a prescription, it's best taken under a doctor's supervision to monitor for possible side effects such as bleeding and gastrointestinal problems.

**Ginkgo.** Derived from the leaves of an Asiatic tree, this extract is believed to have antioxidant properties. It's currently available in Germany for the treatment of dementia and is taken in many countries as a dietary supplement. A 1997 study published in the *Journal of the American Medical Association* reported a modest improvement in people with Alzheimer's who were given a particular extract of ginkgo. Less than 50 percent of the participants completed the trial, however, so the alleged benefits have been difficult to interpret.

Other studies of ginkgo are being performed both as a treatment for Alzheimer's and as a means of prevention. One multicenter trial is comparing the effects of ginkgo and those of a placebo over a period of 6 months. Another trial involves monitoring a group of around 3,000 older adults for 5 years to see if a daily dose of ginkgo will reduce the incidence of dementia among them.

### Neurotrophic agents

Neurotrophic agents are groups of amino acids (polypeptides) that assist in the development and survival of neurons. Some scientists think that introducing these agents into the brain of someone with Alzheimer's disease may help damaged neurons. The following therapies are being investigated:

**Nerve growth factor.** Nerve growth factor (NGF) is a protein that has been shown to enhance the activity of neurons associated with acetylcholine in older animals. It's possible that NGF may do the same in people with Alzheimer's disease. But there have been problems getting NGF to the brain. NGF becomes inactive when taken orally. It's also difficult for NGF to pass through the protective barrier that surrounds the brain (blood-brain barrier), and so NGF can't be introduced intravenously. To overcome these problems, a current phase I study is using a method called gene therapy. Specialized cells (fibroblasts) are taken from the participant's skin and are genetically modified in a laboratory to produce NGF. These cells are then transplanted to the basal nucleus of Meynert, an area of the brain rich in acetylcholine.

**Leteprinim potassium.** Some scientists have developed tiny neurotrophic molecules that are able to cross the blood-brain barrier. One such agent is leteprinim potassium (Neotrofin), also known as AIT-082, which can be taken orally. In preclinical studies, AIT-082 improved memory in both young and old mice. Healthy older adults recently volunteered for a phase I study of the neurotrophic agent. Participants in the treatment group, given increasing doses of AIT-082, did better on some memory and concentration tests than those in the control group who received a placebo. On this first trial, the drug was well tolerated and no significant side effects were observed. Other phase I and phase II trials are now in progress in an attempt to establish the effects of AIT-082.

### Anti-amyloid treatment

As a result of the recent advances in our understanding of beta-amyloid and its potentially toxic accumulation in the brain, many scientists are pursuing ways of removing amyloid aggregations or preventing them from forming. One prominent development is the idea of immunizing against beta-amyloid. Another idea is inhibiting the proteases that snip the amyloid percursor protein that forms amyloid (see page 44).

**AN-1792 vaccine.** In a study published in 1999, researchers announced that they had tested a vaccine, known as AN-1792, on groups of mice genetically programmed (transgenic mice) to develop amyloid plaques in their brains. Two key findings emerged from this research. First, the researchers found strong evidence indicating the vaccine prevented plaque formation in the transgenic mice when they were injected at an early age. Second, there appeared to be a reduction in the number of plaques in older mice injected with the vaccine. Scientists theorize that AN-1792 may trigger a response in the immune system that can remove plaques from the brain. This may occur when anti-beta-amyloid antibodies, created by the immune system, bind to the beta-amyloid and either prevent it from aggregating or accelerate its clearance.

Further vaccine research on transgenic mice revealed improvements in their memory. In December 2000, two independent research teams reported that transgenic mice that had developed memory deficits improved after repeated vaccinations. The mice took part in tests where they swam until they learned the location of an underwater platform. Not only did vaccinated mice perform better on these memory tests than their untreated counterparts, but many also did as well or nearly as well as ordinary mice that were not programmed to develop plaques.

One of the limitations of these animal studies has been that transgenic mice were programmed either to develop plaques or to develop tangles, but no mice were programmed to develop both. A group of researchers recently changed this situation when they crossbred the two lines of mice to create a third line that develops both plaques and tangles. The brain of this type of mouse more closely resembles how Alzheimer's develops in the brain of a human. Having a mouse that exhibits these characteristics will allow researchers to test the vaccine's full effect and perhaps clarify the relationships of plaques and tangles to the disease process that Alzheimer's follows.

Although the AN-1792 vaccine for Alzheimer's disease sounds promising, the question of whether it will work in humans is still unanswered. The human immune system is substantially different from a mouse's. Humans might develop a tolerance to the vaccine, or the vaccine may induce inflammation that didn't occur in the mice. Unfortunately, the first large-scale test of the vaccine in humans caused serious side effects in approximately 5 percent of the participants. As a result, the phase II trial was halted prematurely. Whether any benefits occurred among the remaining participants who received the vaccine is unknown as of April 2002.

**Protease inhibitors.** Now that the actions of the amyloid-clipping enzymes beta-secretase and gamma-secretase are better understood, scientists are working to develop specific protease inhibitors that will reduce secretase activity. The hope is that these will prevent the formation of beta-amyloid and consequently amyloid plaques.

## Using imaging in Alzheimer's research

Imaging techniques have become important tools in the diagnosis of Alzheimer's because they're able to narrow the possible causes of dementia and rule out such sources as strokes and tumors. These imaging techniques have also become increasingly useful in research through their ability to detect changes in brain anatomy and function, often before outward signs and symptoms are detected. Unlike other ways of studying the brain, imaging techniques can provide quantitative measures of how the brain functions over time. This can shed additional light on the progression of a disease such as Alzheimer's.

### Magnetic resonance imaging

Magnetic resonance imaging (MRI) is an imaging technology that provides a picture of the form and structure of the brain (see page 59). Researchers are using MRI to measure the volume of different brain structures that are affected by Alzheimer's, particularly the hippocampus. Several studies have compared brain volume measurements of people with no cognitive impairment with that of people with mild memory difficulties or MCI over a defined period of time. The results indicate that those participants who went on to develop Alzheimer's were the ones who had a greater loss in brain volume during the time of the studies. This suggests that it might be possible to predict Alzheimer's development by observing the rate of brain atrophy (shrinkage). Another study found that the volume of the hippocampus is an accurate predictor of a person's performance on certain cognitive tests. Researchers are also investigating whether MRIs might offer unique information about the progression of Alzheimer's once it has developed in the brain.

## Positron emission tomography

Positron emission tomography (PET) is another technique that can provide images of the brain. A PET scan can detect mild physiological changes in the brain even when no symptoms are evident and before severe damage to brain cells and memory loss occur (see the sidebar on page 59). PET also provides visual images of activity in the brain when a person is asked to read, talk or listen to music. Such uses of PET may help scientists to better understand the progression of Alzheimer's disease in different areas of the brain.

Recent studies have combined the use of genetic testing and PET scanning to examine the brains of middle-age to older adults carrying APOE ε4, a known genetic risk factor for Alzheimer's. Over time, these studies note lower brain functions in the memory and learning regions of the brains of the APOE ε4 carriers, as opposed to those who do not have this version of the APOE gene. Scientists also believe that this method of observation will require fewer candidates and shorter amounts of time than other methods to test potential preventive treatments.

Scientists are also combining PET scans and MRIs to create three-dimensional images of the brain, making it possible for the scientists to measure the rate at which various regions of the brain use, deposit or metabolize certain chemicals.

## Single-photon emission computerized tomography

Single-photon emission computerized tomography (SPECT) is an imaging technique that, similar to PET, detects radioactive emissions within the body and reveals more about the function of the brain rather than its structure. SPECT is used to measure blood flow to various regions of the brain in an attempt to detect those people at risk of developing Alzheimer's.

# Who supports Alzheimer's research?

The federal government, private industry and nonprofit organizations contribute to research on Alzheimer's disease. The National Institute on Aging (NIA) and other parts of the National Institutes of Health (NIH) fund and conduct basic research on the healthy brain and abnormal disease processes. The NIA also established a number of Alzheimer's research programs, including:

- Alzheimer's Disease Centers (ADCs). Research facilities at major medical institutions across the country
- Alzheimer's Disease Cooperative Study (ADCS). A network of 83 research centers in the United States and Canada focusing on potential treatments
- National Alzheimer's Coordinating Center (NACC). Office that coordinates, combines and analyzes data from all 83 centers of the Alzheimer's Disease Cooperative Study network and then makes this information available to Alzheimer's Disease Center facilities and to other research centers
- Drug Discovery for the Treatment Alzheimer's Disease. Research facilities working on possible drug treatments
- Satellite Diagnosis and Treatment Clinics. Research facilities affiliated with the Alzheimer's Disease Centers that focus on recruitment and diversity among study volunteers

In 2001, the NIA awarded $54 million to the ADCS to develop better diagnostic tools and test a variety of drugs designed to delay the progression of Alzheimer's or prevent the disease altogether.

The development of new drugs is an expensive and usually risky venture that mostly takes place in private industry. According to the Pharmaceutical Research and Manufacturers of America Foundation, pharmaceutical companies invested $30.3 billion in the research and development of new drug therapies in 2001. Drugs that may be used for Alzheimer's are considered one of the top three research priorities of the pharmaceutical industry. Non-profit organizations such as the Alzheimer's Association also fund research and work to keep people up-to-date on the latest developments.

# *QUICK* GUIDE
## *for caregivers*

# Quick guide for caregivers

# Activities of daily living

## Bathing and grooming

As Alzheimer's disease progresses, your loved one will go from independently bathing and grooming, to needing reminders to engage in personal care, to requiring hands-on assistance, to being totally dependent on others to provide this care. In-home assistants can be hired to help you and your loved one with these tasks. Many assisted-living facilities and all nursing homes can provide this care. If you're helping your loved one carry out these tasks, here are some tips you might use:

- Provide adequate time for each task, and avoid rushing.
- Try to give simple, one-step commands, and explain your steps.
- Assess the level of assistance that's required daily. For example, can your loved one shave by himself if you set out supplies? Or can he shave by himself if you turn on the razor and put it in his hands? Or does he need you to provide hands-on assistance for the entire task?
- Prepare bathing supplies and bathwater before attempting the task of bathing.
- Make sure the temperature in the room is warm enough to be comfortable without clothing.
- Provide for privacy. If mirrors are distracting, cover or remove them.
- Speak with gentle, reassuring tones.
- Try to maintain a routine. For example, make sure the person has a bath at the same time of day — it doesn't matter at what time, just be consistent with the schedule. Or if a person takes showers, don't vary the routine by occasionally giving the person a sponge bath or a tub bath.
- Install grab bars for safety and reassurance.
- Provide a towel for around the shoulders or on the lap if privacy is a concern for your loved one.
- If your loved one refuses a bath, back off and try again later.

- Ensure adequate lighting, but you can try dimming the light slightly to create a relaxing atmosphere.
- Encourage your loved one to smell the shampoo and soap to trigger a sense of enjoyment.
- Help your loved one feel involved with simple parts of the task, such as washing the face and arms or simply holding an extra washcloth.
- Try singing favorite songs as a distraction.
- Check with a medical supply company for special shower chairs and other equipment that may assist you.
- Spouses might shower with the person.
- Consider a sponge bath or a bed bath using no-rinse soap if your loved one consistently refuses to take a bath.

## Dressing

As Alzheimer's progresses, your loved one will have increasing difficulty with selecting appropriate clothing for the occasion and with putting various articles of clothing on properly. Buttons, zippers, snaps and buckles may cause considerable frustration. Here are some tips that may make everyone's life a little easier:

- To avoid overwhelming your loved one, limit clothing selection. Remove unused or seasonal clothing from closets and dressers.
- Choose appropriate clothing for your loved one for special occasions.
- Hang coordinated outfits together, or buy clothing that will always match.
- Unless the setting is formal, be tolerant of mismatched or stained items or clothing worn inside out.
- It's common for a person with Alzheimer's to layer items of clothing. Generally the person will remove these pieces of extra clothing if he or she becomes too hot or uncomfortable.

- Emphasize comfort over appearance. Look for items that are durable, can be easily cleaned and have easy fasteners or elastic waists. Replace challenging fasteners with Velcro. Add a keychain ring to zippers for easier maneuvering.
- If your loved one wants to wear the same outfit daily, launder it in the evening or buy multiples of the same item.
- Lay out clothing in the order it's put on, for example, undergarments, blouse or shirt, pants, socks and shoes.
- Break down the task of dressing to one step at a time. Demonstrate if necessary.
- Buy clothes a size larger than usual if dressing is difficult.
- For the sake of convenience, avoid dry-clean-only apparel and nylon stockings.
- Undershirts may be used in place of bras if extra support is not required. You may find it difficult to help your loved one put on a bra. Once the strap is fastened, have your loved one lean forward to adjust her breasts into the bra cups.
- Consider the possibility that the person may be in pain if he or she resists moving arms or legs to put on clothing.
- In case of a consistent refusal to change clothes:
  - Provide comfortable outfits such as sweat suits, which can be worn during the day and while sleeping.
  - "Accidentally" spill a bit of water on the clothes to encourage changing into something dry.
  - Modify clothing for easier removal by cutting the seams of pant legs and refastening them with Velcro.

## Eating and nutrition

Although nutrition may have little effect on how Alzheimer's disease progresses, it's important for your loved one to have a balanced, healthy diet. Malnutrition and dehydration, common concerns for people with dementia, may increase confusion and stress, trigger many physical problems and reduce your loved one's ability to cope.

Specific problems are associated with Alzheimer's disease that may inhibit eating. In the early stages of AD, a person, especially one living alone, may forget to eat or may forget how to prepare meals. As the disease progresses, the person may forget table manners and eat from others' plates or out of serving bowls. In some cases, the person loses impulse control and tries to eat anything in sight, including items not intended as food. During the end stages of the disease, he or she may lose the ability to swallow and may experience choking.

Here are some tips to help you meet your loved one's eating and nutritional needs:

### Failing to eat

- Provide reminders to eat. For example, phone your loved one when it's time for a meal.
- Leave a step-by-step list of how to prepare a simple meal if your loved one lives alone.
- Stay with your loved one through the entire meal.
- Demonstrate the steps involved in eating, or give simple, one-step commands.
- Serve simple foods that don't require utensils.
- Omit extra utensils.
- Leave finger foods within easy reach throughout the day.
- Try serving several small meals during the day.
- Make sure the eating area has good lighting.
- Provide adequate time for meals, and avoid rushing.
- Reduce background distractions such as telephone, radio and television.

- Offer foods with varied textures, colors and flavors. Stay with familiar favorites.
- Present foods on attractive table settings of different colors and textures.
- Use contrasting colors to help your loved one locate food. For example, use a blue placemat and white plate with dark foods. Avoid putting a food such as mashed potatoes on a white plate.
- Unless weight is a significant problem, don't discourage eating sweets.
- When using nutritional shakes, blend them with fresh fruit and ice cream to improve the flavor.
- If chewing and swallowing are difficult, use a tasteless food thickener to even the texture of blended foods — see your local pharmacist for this product.
- Try having the person smell lemon or peppermint oils before a meal since this may stimulate appetite.
- Consider a medical checkup to see if depression, ill-fitting dentures, a medical condition or medication possibly causes the decrease in appetite.

**Eating too much**

- Keep food out of sight except at mealtimes.
- Dish food onto plates in the kitchen, and avoid placing serving bowls on the dining room table.
- Cut food into bite-size pieces to avoid choking.
- Remove small nonedible items from the environment.
- Keep poisons in a locked cupboard. Childproof locks are available at hardware stores.
- Exercise patience if the person eats from others' plates.

## Medications

Your loved one may receive recommendations for over-the-counter treatments or get medication prescriptions to treat the symptoms of Alzheimer's disease. He or she may also take medications for other conditions. Giving medications to your loved one may be complicated if he or she takes many pills throughout the day. Here are suggestions that may help if you're responsible for meeting the daily medication needs:

- Create a list of the medications, the dosages and the time you should give each medication. Post the list inside a kitchen cupboard door.
- Use a weekly pillbox to help keep track of whether you have given the medications for the day. You can buy these pillboxes at the pharmacy. If your loved one takes pills more than once a day, have a separate pillbox for each time the person takes medications. For example, write in permanent marker on the outside of the box, "Harold, 8 a.m. pills" or "Harold, noon pills."
- If your loved one lives alone, check the pillbox frequently to make sure he or she is taking the pills correctly. You may need to provide a reminder phone call and stay on the phone while the person takes the medications to ensure he or she doesn't forget.
- Keep a list of common side effects and other information about the medications close at hand.
- Place the phone number for your doctor's office and poison control next to the phone in case of an accidental overdose.
- If your loved one experiences some changes in behavior, demeanor or physical condition, consider whether any medications have recently been changed. Contact your doctor's office if you have concerns.
- Be sure to tell your doctor if you're giving your loved one herbal supplements or other over-the-counter products. These substances may interact with the medications your doctor has prescribed and could cause harmful side effects.

- When a new medication is prescribed, ask your doctor or nurse to provide you with the following information:
    - The name of the drug
    - The dosage
    - The time of day it should be given
    - The purpose of the medication (Don't forget this! Families often have no idea why a medication has been prescribed.)
    - Potential side effects
- Make sure every doctor and specialist your loved one sees is aware of all medications and over-the-counter substances that are being taken.
- Do not change dosages without the consent of your physician.
- Throw out old prescriptions, and don't use medications for anyone other than the person for whom they're prescribed.
- Keep a list of your loved one's medications, dosages and starting dates with you at all times.
- If your loved one refuses a medication or spits it out, try to provide a simple, clear explanation for its purpose. For example, "Mom, here is your blood pressure medication. The doctor said you need to take it for your heart." If she continues to refuse, ask your doctor if you can hide the medication in applesauce, cottage cheese, ice cream or a small amount of juice. You may be able to crush the medication to make it less noticeable. Some medications are available in liquid form.
- Medications that are used to control difficult behaviors can have particularly harmful side effects. Try to use nonmedication interventions as found in this Quick Guide before asking your doctor for medical intervention. Antidepressants tend to be better tolerated and are more helpful than anxiolytic or antipsychotic drugs.

## Home safety and environment

Alzheimer's disease impairs cognitive skills like judgment and problem solving. Caregivers can modify the home environment to help their loved ones stay safe and maneuver within the home as easily as possible. Here are some suggestions for simplifying your living space:

- Keep a list of emergency numbers by all telephones, including poison control, your doctor's office and family contacts.
- Make sure you have a first aid kit, fire extinguisher and working smoke alarms in your home.
- If your loved one is confusing hot and cold faucets, color-code them red and blue. Adjust your home's water heater to 120 degrees to avoid burns.
- Keep poisons, cleaners and medications out of sight, particularly if your loved one is confused about what's edible or is taking medications more frequently than required.
- Some studies show that most people with Alzheimer's will experience at least one fall at some point during the disease process. You may not be able to prevent all falls but to reduce your loved one's risk, consider the following:
  - Get rid of throw rugs or secure the edges with carpet tape.
  - Keep walkways and stairwells free of clutter.
  - Provide adequate lighting in areas of the house that are particularly hard to see.
  - Move electrical cords under furniture or tape to walls.
  - Make sure handrails are available in stairways.
  - Avoid moving furniture, as this may disorient the person and cause a fall.
  - If the person is falling out of bed, consider putting the mattress on the floor.
  - Put non-skid decals on the floor of the bathtub.
  - Install grab bars in the shower and use a specialized shower chair.

- Use small appliances with automatic shut-off systems including the clothes iron, coffeepot and curling iron.
- Cover electrical outlets.
- As Alzheimer's disease progresses, your loved one is at increased risk for wandering away from home. Wandering may be a sign that the person is hungry, tired, bored or needs to use the bathroom. See that all basic needs are being met. Here are some ways to reduce the risk of wandering:
    - Put a slide bolt high on doors to the outside or to stairwells, or use a deadbolt that requires a key. Plastic handle covers that must be squeezed to open a door may also be used. Never leave the person alone when these are in use.
    - Alarms that alert you when a door is being opened can be purchased for a reasonable cost.
    - Some caregivers disguise doors to the outside by covering them with curtains, wallpaper or paint, or by using a "Stop" or "Do not enter" sign.
- Keep a spare key hidden outside your home in case your loved one accidentally locks you out.
- Put a "No solicitation" sign on your door to prevent unwanted visitors.
- Alert neighbors of your loved one's condition so they can help watch for signs that he or she needs help.
- Check the refrigerator for spoiled food your loved one might still eat.
- Store cleaners outside of the kitchen.
- If you are concerned that your loved one should not use sharp or poisonous items, use childproof locks on cupboards and in drawers. These locks are available in hardware stores.
- Keep most-often-used kitchen items in easy-to-reach places.
- Limit stove use if necessary. When not in use, try one of the following:
    - Throw the circuit breaker for the stove.
    - Remove stove knobs.
    - Use a plastic bubble lens to cover stove knobs.
    - Unplug the stove.

- Consider removing metal bowls from the kitchen that may start a fire if placed in the microwave.
- Keep nightlights in hallways, bathroom and bedrooms. You might even want to leave a light on in the bathroom all night.
- Store electrical appliances outside the bathroom.
- Check medicine cabinet for toxic items.
- Try using a colored toilet seat if the person is having difficulty seeing the toilet.

## Questions to ask if you are concerned about your loved one staying alone:

Does the person:
- become confused or unpredictable under stress?
- recognize a dangerous situation like fire or cold?
- know how to use a phone in an emergency?
- know how to get help?
- stay content within the home?
- wander and become disoriented?
- show signs of agitation, anxiety or depression when left alone?
- attempt to pursue hobbies that need supervision, like cooking, appliance repair, sewing or woodworking?
- give freely to people asking for money?

These questions may help you determine if your loved one should be left alone. Ask other family members or friends for their perspective, but remember the primary caregiver usually has the most valuable insight based on daily contact with the person.

## Toileting and incontinence

Incontinence may occur for a variety of reasons. If this is a new behavior, consider what's caused this change. Has your loved one forgotten where the bathroom is located? Is your loved one having difficulty with unfastening clothing? Is there a medical reason for the incontinence, for example, a bladder infection, medication change or prostate difficulty? If none of these reasons appears to be causing the incontinence, it may be occurring as a result of the disease process. Here are some ways to help you cope:

- Put a picture of a toilet and a sign that reads *toilet* on the bathroom door. Avoid the word *restroom* or *bathroom* which may be taken literally.
- Leave the door to the bathroom open and a light on to help your loved one easily locate the room, particularly at night.
- Watch for nonverbal signs that indicate your loved one needs to use the toilet. He or she may not recognize the feeling of a full bladder or lack the verbal skills to state this need. You may find your loved one pulls on his or her pants, paces or shows other signs of agitation.
- Provide frequent reminders to use the toilet. Generally a pattern of every 1 to 2 hours works well. You may need to bring the person to the bathroom and provide hands-on assistance to help unfasten clothing.
- Some caregivers put reflective tape on the floor in the shape of arrows that point to the location of the bathroom.
- Avoid clothing with complicated fasteners, like button-fly jeans. Elastic waistbands usually work well. Women may fare better with knee-high stockings instead of regular pantyhose.
- Dehydration is fairly common for people with dementia. Don't decrease fluids unless the person is drinking vast amounts of liquids — more than 8 to 10 glasses in a day. Withholding fluids may actually increase incontinence because of the risk of dehydration. However, you may want to discourage more than

one beverage after dinner to decrease nighttime incontinence.

- A new episode of incontinence should be evaluated by a medical practitioner. Specifically, ask for a test to determine if your loved one has a urinary tract or bladder infection.
- A variety of incontinence products are available at your local drug store. Small pads similar to those used for menstruation may be placed in underpants if your loved one is experiencing urinary incontinence only. Briefs worn instead of underwear are best if your loved one has fecal incontinence or if the small pads are not adequately holding the urine. Briefs may have reusable straps with buttons or Velcro, or tape tabs similar to disposable diapers. Depending on their incontinence pattern, some people wear pads during the day and briefs at night. Your doctor, nurse or pharmacist can help determine which product is best for your loved one.
- Use a plastic or rubber pad under a fitted bed sheet for nighttime incontinence. Disposable Chux pads with a white cotton top and blue plastic underside can also be used to reduce frequent bed changes. Fold a top sheet into thirds and place over the Chux for added comfort.
- At night, you may find it is easier to change incontinence products while the person is in bed rather than in the bathroom. During the day, changing may be easiest when the person is seated on the toilet.

## Travel and transporting outside the home

Deciding to travel or attend events outside the familiar home environment grows increasingly difficult as Alzheimer's progresses. Here are some suggestions for making those times easier if you decide to attempt a trip:

- If you are uncertain how your loved one will react to a long trip, try daylong or overnight trips beforehand.

- Alert any travel or hospitality staff ahead of time that your loved one has dementia. Special arrangements can be made to board planes early or to use wheelchairs to alleviate fatigue in places that involve a lot of walking.
- Simplify your vacation plans. Avoid trying to cram too many activities into a single day and try to keep changes throughout the day to a minimum. Plan for rest periods between activities and provide a quiet haven for your loved one to retreat to if necessary.
- Your loved one may become confused about when the trip will take place and what preparations are required. You may find it easier not to talk about the trip until just prior to leaving — like the day before. Provide reassurance: "Tomorrow we're going to visit our daughter Susan in Wisconsin. Don't worry, we've packed everything we need and I'll be with you the whole time."
- Before leaving home, register for the Safe Return Program (see page 188). Contact the Alzheimer's Association for more information.
- You may find it helpful to alert people outside the home of your loved one's condition. Bring a small card with you that says, "The person with me has Alzheimer's disease. Thank you for your patience." Show the card to restaurant servers, flight attendants, cashiers and others who should be aware of your situation.
- Consider bringing a second person to assist you. This may be particularly helpful at locations with public restrooms if you and the care recipient are not of the same sex.
- Create a backup plan in case your loved one needs to return home quickly.
- Keep passports, traveler's checks and other important papers with you. Give your loved one a small amount of money for a wallet or purse, but no more than you would be comfortable losing if he or she misplaced it.
- Bring a list of medications, insurance information and emergency contacts. Compile a list of medical facilities for each destination — available from the Alzheimer's Association.

- Give an itinerary and contact information to your family.
- Bring snacks and simple, fun activities like magazines with bright colorful pictures, audiotapes, a small photo album or a deck of cards.
- Have your loved one wear comfortable shoes and familiar clothes.
- On airplanes or trains, take the aisle seat and have your loved one sit inside to control for wandering. A window seat may help keep your loved one engaged.
- Try to keep meals consistent with home, including time of day and types of food. If crowded restaurants confuse your loved one, consider taking advantage of room service.
- Bring a waterproof sheet and extra pads if your loved one has experienced incontinence.
- Caregivers often find that trips with their loved ones constitute a working vacation. The person with Alzheimer's may experience anxiety away from home and then quickly forget about the trip afterward. Using respite care that allows your loved one to stay home while you travel may be easier for both of you.

QUICK
GUIDE

## Difficult moods and behaviors

## Aggression

Aggressive behavior involves confrontation or a belligerent action against someone or something. Try to calm feelings of anger and frustration before they can lead to aggression. A noisy environment or poor communication skills may exacerbate the strong emotions. If aggression occurs, the following tips may help in your response:

- If your loved one becomes verbally aggressive, try not to take it personally. Remember, the disease, not the person, is causing this behavior.
- Avoid confronting your loved one. Speak in a soothing, quiet tone of voice. Be positive and reassuring. Try not to overreact or startle your loved one, which may only increase agitation.
- Back away from physical aggression. It may help to say, "Please don't hurt me" or "Please stop." Remove all people and animals from the room until your loved one calms down.
- Minimize restraining your loved one — for example by holding the person's hands or arms — if he or she becomes aggressive. This may only increase frustration. However, do what you must to be safe.
- If you are concerned about aggression, remove heavy or sharp objects from the environment. Keep them out of sight.
- Consider the immediate cause of aggression. What seemed to trigger the incident? Reflect on how removing this trigger might prevent further incidents.
- Some aggressive incidents may not be related to the environment and may need to be treated with medication. Consider whether your loved one may be depressed since depression sometimes causes aggressive behavior.

## Anger or irritation

Anger is a strong emotional response that often shows itself in a desire to fight back at the cause of displeasure. Becoming irritable is a somewhat milder response. Sometimes if your loved one's feelings of anxiety and frustration go unacknowledged, his or her emotions can escalate into anger.

- Use a gentle, supportive approach when interacting with your loved one. Acknowledge the feelings the person is experiencing.
- Simplify tasks for your loved one and provide instructions one step at a time.
- Speak slowly and clearly and don't talk about your loved one as if the person wasn't there. Misinterpreting a conversation may cause anger.
- Sudden noises or movements may startle your loved one and quickly lead to anger. Make sure you're in sight before touching the person.
- Ask only one question at a time and try not to contradict or scold your loved one. Step in subtly to assist if the person is struggling with a task such as dressing or cooking.
- Be aware of the age-appropriateness of activities you give your loved one to do. The person may become angry if engaged in a child-like task.
- Back off and give your loved one time to cool down if he or she becomes angry. It also may be helpful to go for a walk together to help the person burn off steam.
- Keep a log showing when angry incidents occur, particularly if you're uncertain of the trigger. Look for patterns such as time of day, place or activity.
- Anger or irritation may be a sign of depression. Ask your doctor for assistance if these emotions occur regularly. The depression associated with dementia may occur with or without crying spells.

- Consider whether your loved one is sleep deprived. Anger may result from fatigue.
- Physical discomfort may cause anger. Consider whether your loved one is in pain, ill, constipated or hungry or whether he or she needs to use the bathroom.
- Consider whether your loved one has recently changed medications. Side effects of certain drugs may include drastic mood changes.
- Distract your loved one with a favorite activity or snack.
- Try quiet music or reassuring touch to soothe angry feelings.

## Anxiety or frustration

Anxiety involves an extreme sense of fear about an impending event, about something that's going to happen in the future. The dangers can be real or imagined. Anxiety may occur for a variety of reasons. A person with Alzheimer's may worry needlessly about family, work and things left undone, even if these are no longer responsibilities. Someone with anxiety may feel helpless, inadequate, restless and unable to sleep.

People who are frustrated seem to be in a chronic state of tension or insecurity. The feelings are caused by an inability to resolve problems or fulfill needs. To reduce frustration, you can try to anticipate troublesome incidents before they occur. However, it's important to remember that frustration is a natural response to the mental and physical losses caused by Alzheimer's disease and you'll not be able to prevent all occurrences.

**If your loved one is feeling anxiety:**

- Focus on ways to reassure your loved one. Take concerns seriously. The person truly believes these worries are valid even if they seem unfounded to you.
- Join your loved one in his or her current understanding of the world. Try to provide an explanation that makes sense in this

reality and at the same time gives reassurance and relief. The truth in what you say is not as important as your loved one's emotional response to your explanation.

- If your loved one worries about a spouse (who is deceased), perhaps you can say that the spouse has run to the store or is at work.
- If your loved one worries about a job (which he or she no longer has), perhaps you can say that an employer called to say there is no need to come to work today.

- Try to express the reality of a situation gently, but do so only if your loved one can be reassured. Don't try to assert the truth if it's upsetting or if your loved one doesn't believe what you're saying.
- You may find it helpful to provide a tangible backup for your explanation. Try pretending to talk on the phone to an employer or have your loved one talk to a family member. Present a written phone message or letter giving a reassuring message. It's important to validate your loved one's feelings to let the person know you care and understand: "Mom, I know you're really upset about this."
- Reminisce about any past memories your loved one may bring up. Use a photo album to frame your discussion.
- Distract your loved one with an enjoyable activity that refocuses his or her attention on something positive. You will generally find it works best to first join the person's world to reassure and validate his or her emotions before attempting such a distraction.

**If your loved one is feeling frustrated:**
- Allow your loved one to do as much as possible with the least amount of assistance.
- Try not to worry about the way things should be done. Refrain from correcting your loved one if the person is not endangering himself or herself or others.
- Allow more time to accomplish everyday caregiving tasks to avoid rushing your loved one.
- Because your loved one can't do as much doesn't mean he or

she should stop attempting the activity. Strive for a balance between periods of rest and activity. Minimize activity later in the day when the person is more likely to be fatigued.

- Check to see if too much noise and activity in the environment might be causing frustration. Limit or turn off the television or radio and set aside a quiet room for your loved one to rest.
- Change can increase confusion and frustration. Try to maintain a consistent routine and avoid change as much as possible.
- Adapt your expectations as the disease progresses. For example, leaving a familiar home environment may become overwhelming and frightening for your loved one in late stages of the disease. You may not be able to plan as many away-from-home activities as you had at earlier stages.
- Be aware of how your own emotions may affect and possibly frustrate your loved one. Try to be calm and reassuring.

## Apathy or depression

Apathy is the difficult behavior most commonly reported by Alzheimer's caregivers. The feeling is characterized by indifference, often in situations that would normally arouse strong feelings or reactions. Apathy may also include a lack of motivation, periods of sitting and staring blankly and a sense of disengagement from the world. Depression is also common among people with Alzheimer's (see page 37). Signs and symptoms of depression include anger and irritability, frequent crying spells, changes in appetite and sleep patterns and apathy. Here are some considerations:

- Try to engage your loved one in favorite activities. Use old photo albums, home videos or pictures of children and baby animals. Try to reminisce about the past, which your loved one is more likely to be able to do, rather than discuss recent events.

- Play music with a strong tempo, such as big band music or marches, to encourage your loved one to clap or stomp his or her feet. But be aware of any adverse reaction if the music is too loud or disruptive.
- Acknowledge your loved one's feelings. He or she may be experiencing grief over physical and mental losses due to Alzheimer's or for loved ones who have died.
- Use simple humor to lighten the load of Alzheimer's disease for both of you. A book of simple jokes or videos of old television comedies may bring some laughter.
- Talk to your doctor if you see signs of depression in your loved one. Antidepressant medications are safe and effective with minimal side effects. Your doctor may try various drugs and dosages in order to find what works best for the person.
- Talk therapy or group therapy is generally not recommended for people with Alzheimer's disease, especially after the early stage. In order to be effective, this type of therapy requires the ability to process and remember information. Instead, consider elder care programs that can engage your loved one in activities and socialization with other people.

## Clinging or making demands

Clinging often occurs as a result of anxiety or fear of abandonment. Your loved one may rely on you completely to help maneuver through the day. Even the simplest tasks may involve your participation. Your loved one may also watch your moods and expressions for clues on how to react to situations.

- Provide lots of verbal reassurance that everything is OK.
- Try to meet requests in an appropriate, acceptable way. For example, you might agree to go with your loved one, who wants to go to happy hour for drinks, but take him or her instead out for ice cream. Be creative and try to have fun.
- Avoid using the *no* word. You may even say yes to demands that you'll eventually steer away from.
- Consider patterns that may trigger anxiety, such as a particular environment or time of day. Try to determine what helps calm your loved one.
- Provide an activity to distract your loved one. A repetitive task may be particularly useful, such as folding towels, sweeping floors, raking leaves or winding yarn. You may even give the person a stick of gum or a snack to focus on.
- Give your loved one objects that have a calming effect — perhaps a stuffed animal, fuzzy blanket or cup of herbal tea — or play soothing music.
- Make sure you find some time for yourself amidst the person's demands. You may need to arrange respite care at least once a week, if not more.
- Lock the door to give yourself privacy in the bathroom. If your loved one is capable of being alone, set a timer and say, "I'll be back when the timer goes off."
- Ask for advice and assistance from a caregiver support group. Clinging behavior can be particularly taxing for caregivers and you'll need extra support.

GUIDE

## Delusions, suspicion or paranoia

Delusions are false beliefs that a person may have which you can't change or modify, no matter how much reasoning you apply. Delusions often occur with Alzheimer's disease, and they may cause your loved one to become suspicious and paranoid. Doubt and a lack of trust characterize suspicion. For example, your loved one may forget where she placed her purse and assumes someone has stolen it. Often she will believe whoever is in the house has taken the missing item, or she may think someone has entered the home to steal it. Your loved one may also experience paranoia, believing, for example, that people are "out to get me." Here are some tips to help you cope with these behaviors:

- Try not to take it personally if suspicion is directed at you. Remember that these feelings are a result of the disease. Your loved one is not intentionally treating you this way.
- If your loved one is adamant about his or her concerns, indicate that you take the concerns seriously. Don't dwell on negative feelings because this may only make the feelings worse.
- Rather than argue with your loved one about whether a delusion is real — for example, whether an item has been stolen or not — respond to his or her emotional tone. The fear, anger and frustration are very real, even if the event that triggered the emotions isn't. Assure your loved one that you understand these feelings and provide comfort: "I'm sorry your purse is missing. You sound very upset. Let's look for it together."
- Search for missing items with your loved one. If he or she doesn't allow you to look in certain places, for example in dresser drawers or under a mattress, wait until your loved one is out of the house or otherwise occupied.
- Keep duplicates available of items your loved one tends to hide. For example, have two or three purses or wallets ready to substitute for the one that's disappeared. Put old copies of identification and other reassuring items in them.

- Alzheimer's disease does make your loved one vulnerable to financial abuse, so consider whether he or she is actually reporting a true occurrence.
- When your loved one is experiencing paranoia — for example, about a spouse's faithfulness — encourage him or her to express those concerns. Try not to contradict. Provide a simple, reassuring response: "I'm sorry you've been concerned, but I love you very much and always will." After reassuring, try to switch the focus to a distracting activity.

## Hallucinations or misperceptions

A hallucination is seeing or hearing something that's not there, such as seeing a child in what is an empty backyard or hearing disconnected voices. The person may reach out to touch or grab whatever it is he or she sees. A misperception is seeing an object and mistaking it for something else, such as seeing a chair and thinking it's an animal or trying to pick up the flowers that are a pattern in the carpet. Caregivers should try to distinguish carefully between hallucinations and misperceptions in someone with Alzheimer's disease. Misperceptions are generally harmless. Hallucinations may be harmless but may also indicate a reaction to medication or an illness. Here are some considerations for caregivers:

- Try to determine if your loved one is actually seeing or hearing something that's not there. He or she may also be experiencing a delusion, which is a false belief. Or the person may be misremembering, which is an error in remembering — for example, recounting a conversation that didn't occur. Both delusions and misremembering are common in Alzheimer's. Hallucinations aren't.
- Remember that a hallucination is very real for the person who experiences it. Don't try to convince your loved one that the hallucination doesn't exist.

- Approach a hallucinating person cautiously. Try not to startle or frighten your loved one.
- If your loved one asks if you see or hear something, be honest but gentle: "I didn't hear anything, but I know you're frightened. I'll check the house to make sure everything is OK."
- Assess whether the hallucination is upsetting. Your loved one may not be concerned by what he or she sees. If the person isn't disturbed, treating the hallucination may not be necessary.
- Offer assistance and validate feelings. For example, if your loved one is upset by the hallucination, you might say, "I know this is bothering you. Let me see if I can help." After acknowledging your loved one's concerns, try to distract him or her with an enjoyable activity.
- Some medications may cause hallucinations. Illnesses such as viral infections may also cause hallucinations, especially if the illness occurs suddenly and is severe. Check with your doctor to determine whether either of these potential causes is involved.
- Your doctor may recommend a medication to treat hallucinations, but the side effects may cause additional problems. You may want to consider medication only if your loved one is disturbed by the hallucination.
- Try to explain misinterpretations. You might say, "Yes, that does look like a person over there, but it's just a coat rack. See?" If the misinterpretation is not upsetting, you may not need to explain.
- Mirrors may become confusing and misinterpreted as a second person in the room. Cover or remove mirrors if they're disturbing. Some people with Alzheimer's disease actually find mirrors comforting and may speak to the reflection as though it's a friend.
- Make sure rooms are well lit, especially at night, to reduce misinterpretations.
- Ask yourself if your loved one is experiencing hearing or vision changes that may contribute to the misperceptions. Could these sensory changes be treated to help the situation?

## Hiding things

People with Alzheimer's disease may hide objects in unusual places. This behavior occurs for a variety of reasons. Your loved one may hide items to prevent them from being stolen. The person may be concerned that he or she won't be able to find the items later and so tucks them away for safe keeping. The behavior may be reassuring if the person hoards objects he or she finds comforting. Your loved one may also collect items in the belief that he or she is still providing for the family. Here are some ways to cope with this behavior:

- Because hoarding may be a form of reassurance, don't discourage this behavior. Provide safe, appropriate objects for the purpose of being hidden or tucked away. Garage sales and thrift stores are often good places to buy harmless items to leave out for hoarding.
- Remember not to give your loved one anything you don't want to lose. Keep important cards and papers safely stored. Only leave a few dollars or some change in a purse or wallet.
- If your loved one takes something you need, try to offer something in exchange. For example, if the person takes your car keys, try to trade with a set of spare keys. Watch to see where items are hidden to retrieve them later.
- Objects may be hidden in unusual places such as in the oven, in the refrigerator or under a mattress. Your loved one may wrap a hearing aid in a napkin to throw in the garbage or tuck it inside a pants pocket. Check inside appliances before turning them on and inside wastebaskets before emptying them. Look in clothes pockets before doing a wash.
- You may need to clean out hiding places on a regular basis, especially if your loved one hoards food.
- To reduce the number of places to search when an important item is missing, lock cupboards, drawers, closets and extra rooms. Childproof drawer and cupboard locks are available at

your local hardware store. Provide alternative hiding places such as large handbags.

## Inappropriate sexual behavior

Sexual needs and feelings are generally a natural part of an adult's life and they may not disappear during the disease process. Some behavior exhibited by a person with Alzheimer's may be sexual in nature, but often this behavior is misinterpreted. A lack of inhibition may cause your loved one to touch his or her genitals or undress in response to non-sexual needs, such as feeling uncomfortable or needing to use the bathroom. You may need to discreetly remove your loved one from public space. Here are some other ideas to consider should this kind of behavior arise:

- Try to determine whether your loved one is responding to physical discomfort. He or she may have a sore genital area from incontinence pads. Or perhaps the person is overdressed and too warm.
- Your loved one may be responding to what feels good. The behavior may be a way to self-stimulate.
- Consider whether your loved one is experiencing depression.
- Your loved one continues to need intimacy and physical affection. Increase appropriate touch unless it's too stimulating. Give your loved one a backrub, massage hands with lotion, provide a manicure or brush hair.
- Offer objects to touch and hold such as stuffed animals, fabric swatches, foam balls and feather dusters.
- Caregivers often lose sexual interest in the person as the disease progresses. You're under no obligation to continue sexual encounters with your loved one. It may help to sleep in separate beds.
- If your loved one is making unwanted advances to you, give a calm but firm response. Don't overreact or confront. Say no or

gently redirect him or her to another activity. As noted above, you're not obligated to engage in any unwanted sexual activity. Protect yourself if necessary. Leave the room until the person has calmed down.

- If your loved one is making sexual advances to others, it may be due to mistaking them for a spouse. Try not to take it personally or as a rejection of your relationship. A person to whom the advances are directed may help by saying, "I do look like Mary but I'm your friend Ginny. It's good to be with you today."
- If your loved one is exposing his or her genitals, encourage using the bathroom on a regular basis. Consider using overalls or other clothes that slow down the process of disrobing but then be sure to help him or her use the bathroom frequently.
- Cover your loved one's lap with a pillow or blanket when seated in a chair if he or she is engaging in public masturbation, or bring the person to a private area. Don't feel the need to discourage masturbation unless you believe it's caused by boredom or it's causing skin breakdown.

## Repeated questions or actions

Due to memory loss, a person with Alzheimer's may not realize that he or she is repeating an action or asking the same question over and over again. Repetition may also be caused by anxiety or misunderstanding.

- Answer questions simply. If your loved one asks the same question repeatedly and you tire of answering, write the answer on a note card and hand it to the person to reinforce your answer.
- Try to focus on the meaning behind a repeated question. If your loved one is worried about a parent or a home, reminisce about the past and use a photo album if one is available.

- Even if you can't determine what your loved one is anxious about, give some general reassurance: "It's going to be OK."
- Repetitive actions may also be an attempt to self-stimulate. Give your loved one a task such as sweeping, wiping counters, tearing newspapers or sanding wood. Occupy the person's hands with foam balls, pieces of fabric or other items that provide sensory stimulation.
- If your loved one asks repeatedly to go home, remove any triggers the person might associate with leaving, such as coats, hats and suitcases.
- Some medications have a side effect called *tardive dyskinesia*, which causes mouth movements, jerking and lip smacking. Check with your doctor to determine whether medications may be causing repetitive actions.

## Restlessness or wandering

Wandering may include pacing in the home, walking aimlessly from place to place or leaving the house. There are many causes for wandering, including an unsettled environment, physical discomfort, frustration, boredom, or physical changes in the brain. Due to confusion, your loved one may be looking for a family member or attempting to perform what was once a career-related task. If you are concerned about wandering, you may wish to register the person in the Safe Return Program (see page 188). Here are other considerations:

- Consider the reasons why your loved one might be restless. Is there too much noise in the environment? Is the person engaged in an activity that's too difficult? Is the person bored? Is a medication causing restlessness?
- Watch for patterns that may indicate a certain time of day or an activity that's causing the behavior. Your loved one may also be indicating a need such as hunger, fatigue, needing to use the bathroom, or being lonely or afraid.

- Frequent pacing may cause dehydration. Help your loved one stay hydrated by offering plenty of water throughout the day.
- Take your loved one on frequent walks or exercise together.
- Involve your loved one in activities related to former jobs. Physical tasks are also helpful, such as cooking, cleaning, sweeping and raking.
- Reduce beverages containing caffeine, which may add to restlessness.
- Decrease background noise and excessive stimulation that may cause your loved one to flee. Have a quiet room available during large gatherings.
- If your loved one is asking to go home, take a car ride, walk around the block or go out for a treat.
- Consider whether the wandering is truly a problem. It may not be worth trying to change. Some medications reduce wandering, but these may render your loved one immobile. You may want to avoid medications unless the person is extremely anxious or agitated.
- Rather than discouraging wandering, try to make it safer for your loved one. Keep wandering paths clear of objects that the person could trip over.
- Put up signs pointing to the bathroom and bedroom if your loved one seems confused or lost.
- Keep nightlights in bedrooms, hallways and bathrooms.
- Lock doors to dangerous stairwells.
- Remove triggers that may cause your loved one to believe that it's time to leave, such as coats, hats and suitcases.
- Alert neighbors of your loved one's disease. People are more likely to lend assistance or alert you to any unusual behavior if they know what's happening.
- Consider ways to secure the home if your loved one is trying to leave frequently. Use pressure mat alarms — available at electronics and pet stores — or put bells on doors leading to the outside. Childproof locks and squeeze handles may also be helpful. Some caregivers put deadbolts that require keys on outside doors or place slide bolts out of the person's reach. Never leave your loved one at home alone when using these measures.

- If possible, put a locked fence around your yard to create a safe wandering area outdoors.
- If your loved one lives in a care facility, it is not uncommon for the person to follow staff as they leave at the end of their shift. Encourage the staff to leave quietly without saying goodbye.

## Sleep disturbance

Disrupted sleep patterns are common in people with Alzheimer's disease. Sleep disturbances may be caused by the progressive dementia or by illness, medications or a poorly adapted environment. Be careful of sleep medications, which may only make confusion worse. If your loved one is having difficulty sleeping, consider some of the following techniques:

- Try to maintain a regular bedtime as a part of the daily routine. Reassure your loved one that everything is OK.
- Indicate to your loved one that it's bedtime. Yawn, stretch and say, "I'm sleepy." Turn off the lights together as a bedtime ritual.
- Avoid discussing plans for tomorrow before bed. People with Alzheimer's often confuse time and may start to worry.
- Avoid loud, stimulating television before bedtime. Instead, try reading aloud, playing soft, soothing music or offering a light snack to help calm your loved one.
- Encourage your loved one to use the bathroom before bedtime.
- If changing into pajamas is upsetting for your loved one, use a cotton sweatsuit that can be worn day and night.
- Allow your loved one to sleep wherever he or she prefers, including a recliner chair or couch.
- Give the person activities to do in the night if sleep seems unlikely.
- Avoid giving the person alcohol or caffeine, especially late in the day. But be aware that quitting caffeine abruptly can cause headaches and irritability.

- Encourage your loved one to exercise regularly, including taking walks and doing housework, to burn off excess emotions.
- Consider any medication changes that might cause restlessness or sleep problems.
- If background noise is keeping your loved one from sleeping, try using a white-noise generator that creates a quiet hum to counteract the noise.
- Don't discourage napping during the day, especially if it's the only sleep your loved one gets. It's better to get sleep during the day rather than get no sleep at all.
- Excessive sleep is generally not a problem unless it's caused by depression, boredom or medications.

## Stubbornness or lack of cooperation

A person with Alzheimer's disease may sometimes refuse to obey simple requests. He or she may not be willing to participate in activities such as bathing or taking medications. Here are some techniques that may work when dealing with stubbornness.

- If your loved one refuses to do something, back off and try again later using a different approach. Try to stay flexible. Generally, nothing has to be done immediately. You're capable of adapting to situations more than your loved one is.
- Try performing difficult tasks when your loved one is most alert. For example, bathe after breakfast rather than immediately upon waking. Or perhaps you may find the reverse works better — it may be easier to attempt difficult tasks when he or she is groggy and less likely to struggle.
- You may find it unnecessary to announce your intention ahead of time. Go for a walk through the house and just happen to stop in the bathroom. Be natural about tasks. A simple "Come with me" may work better than explaining that your loved one is about to get a bath.

- Don't ask questions that can be answered with a yes or no. Simply state "It's time for a bath" rather than "Do you want a bath?"
- Offer positive reinforcement. For example, you might say, "After your bath, we'll have a piece of pie." Follow through on such promises.
- Have an official-looking doctor's order to show for certain difficult tasks.
- Try to make things fun. If you have a look of dread on your face, your loved one will probably anticipate an unpleasant experience. Try to consider each attempt a fresh start.
- Use music or snacks to make the experience more enjoyable for both of you. Try to maintain a sense of humor.

## Difficult issues or decisions

## Choosing a new living arrangement

Your community may have a variety of housing options available for your loved one, including alternative housing, assisted-living facilities and nursing homes or skilled care facilities. How do you choose which option is right for your family? Consider the following:

- Find out how many options are available in your community. Your choices may be limited in rural areas. Decide how far you're willing to travel.
- Determine how you'll pay for care by consulting a financial planner or social worker. Find out what payment options are available at your local facilities. This will save you time from exploring options that aren't financially feasible.
- Determine what needs your loved one is experiencing. Are they activities of daily living, companionship, help with walking or with taking medication, or a secured building to prevent wandering? Match your loved one's needs to the services available in the facilities in which you're interested.
- Arrange tours of more than one facility, if possible. Try to visit each site more than once and at different times during the day. As you tour, try to do the following:
  - Watch how the staff members interact with residents. Do the staff members smile? Do they call residents by name?
  - Notice if activities are occurring. If not, is it a rest time?
  - Does the facility seem short-staffed? Do the staff members seem overly rushed?
  - Ask to see a meal schedule. Observe a mealtime. Do the staff members interact with residents during meals?
  - Ask for the home's philosophy of dementia care. How do the staff members handle challenging behaviors? Is the facility safe for wandering?
  - Learn about the admission process. Ask for specific admission and discharge criteria. Does the home have a

waiting list? How long does it generally take for a bed to become available?

- Check to see what payment options are available. Are there additional fees for additional services?

- Decide on your top choice or choices. Ask about putting your loved one on their waiting lists. Some facilities may ask you to make a down payment when you do this. But many others won't require you to make a deposit at this time. Under no circumstances are you obligated to take a room when it becomes available, even if you're on the waiting list.

- Find out about preparing an application and other paperwork ahead of time. Prior contact with the admissions staff can help ease the placement process in case of an emergency.

## Moving day

Once you've decided on a new living arrangement, you can begin the process of helping your loved one adjust to the new environment. Here are some tips for handling the move:

- Share with your loved one as much or as little information as you deem appropriate about the move. Experts vary on advice to families about the decision of what and how much to say. You know your loved one best. What's most important is that you do what you feel is best for your situation. There's no one correct way to handle the process.

- You may consider informing your loved one on the day of the move, since the person will usually forget if told earlier.

- Keep the statement simple: "Mom, today you're moving to a new home."

- Avoid providing too much explanation. For one thing, lengthy explanations are usually not understood and often lead to frustration. For another, they often end up as an argument. You're not likely to convince your loved one of the need to move to a care facility.

  - Frame the explanation for the move in terms the person will understand. Use statements such as, "We want you to be safe, and I'm sure you want that too," or "The home is going to help you make new friends."

- Thank your loved one for "understanding why the move is important."

- Acknowledge your loved one's feelings of pain, anger, grief and loss. You may find it helpful to apologize. Once you've acknowledged painful feelings, try to distract the person with a favorite activity, snack or music.

- Try to stay calm and reassuring. Sometimes, families discover the process is harder for them than it is for the person with Alzheimer's. Your loved one may watch you closely for signs that the situation is safe. If the family is tense, the person may sense this and become anxious.

- Have confidence in your decision. Over 90 percent of people with Alzheimer's eventually live in nursing homes or assisted-living facilities.

- Be aware that Monday through Thursday tend to be the best days for moving. Homes are more likely to be fully staffed on these days. Fridays may be hectic and are too close to the weekend, when there are more visitors.

- If possible, bring your loved one to the new home before lunch or dinner. The meal provides a good excuse for leaving. Some families tell the person they're leaving, while others slip out without saying a goodbye. Use your judgment and work with staff to decide what's best in your situation.

- Ask the admissions staff for advice on moving day. The staff has probably helped many families through this difficult process. You're an expert on your loved one. Work together to create a plan.

- Think about decorating the new living quarters before the move. Put familiar items like photographs and knickknacks in the room to give a sense of identity, security and comfort.

- Try to fill out paperwork in advance so you can focus your attention on reassuring your loved one.

- Decide with the staff ahead of time how long you'll stay with your loved one. Hovering over the person may provide a sense of security, but may not allow for him or her to become acclimated to the environment. Your loved one and the staff need some time to become familiar with each other.

- Bring a photo album or scrapbook with pictures and information about your loved one's life. Include important events, people and hobbies. You may also want to leave a video or audio recording of your voice for the staff to play, giving reassuring messages to your loved one.
- Help the staff get to know your loved one by providing information about current care needs and your loved one's personal history. A written list is more likely to be passed along to all staff, as opposed to telling one staff member who may not have the opportunity to share the information with all those who work with your loved one.
- Be gentle with yourself. This is often the most difficult thing you'll ever do with a family member. Take some time to do what you need to feel better.

## Visiting the nursing home or assisted-living facility

- Bear in mind that you're not required to protect the staff from your loved one's difficult behaviors or to continue providing care for your loved one after the move. You're now part of a team of caregivers. Allow the staff to take over some aspects of care. Focus on enjoying visits and providing love, comfort and reassurance when you visit.
- Work with the staff to determine when and how often to visit your loved one. Make sure you use this new arrangement as an opportunity to get a break from caregiving.
- When you visit, expect there may be changes. The new home is a change in environment. It's naturally a challenge getting used to a new place. With time, your loved one will almost always adjust.
- Your loved one usually cannot remember how often you visit or for how long. Expect to hear "Where have you been?" or "Why don't you ever visit me?" no matter how long it has been between visits.
- When it's time to leave, family members may know the best way to say goodbye. A simple "Goodbye, Mom. I have some errands to do. I'll come back soon" is usually best.
- Giving a personal item such as a scarf or cap to "keep for me until I come back" may be reassuring.

## GUIDE

## Deciding about surgery and medical treatments

When your loved one has received a diagnosis of Alzheimer's disease, it may be difficult deciding whether to treat other conditions that require certain kinds of interventions, such as heart surgery or chemotherapy. Here are some considerations:

- Doctors who specialize in a particular field of medicine, such as cardiology or cancer, may recommend treatments for the conditions in which they specialize. When an invasive treatment has been recommended, you may also want to discuss the options with a general practitioner or neurologist.
- General anesthesia, which is used to render a person unconscious during certain surgeries, usually makes cognitive impairment worse. Sometimes people bounce back from the decline, but this isn't often the case. Ask your doctor if local or spinal anesthesia is possible instead.
- Ask the specialist the following questions to help you make a well-informed decision:
  - What is the goal of the treatment?
  - What benefits could the treatment provide?
  - Would the treatment affect the person's cognitive skills?
  - How may the treatment likely affect the person's quality of life?
  - Is the person likely to experience pain or nausea from the treatment?
  - How frightening or confusing might the treatment be for the person?
- Use the responses from the questions above to help you weigh the benefits of treatment against the negative aspects. For example, electroconvulsive therapy (ECT) for depression may impair your loved one's memory but his or her quality of life may be better because mood has improved. Certain surgeries may lengthen the person's life but decrease the quality of life because of pain or diminished cognitive skills from anesthesia.

- Consider your goals in caregiving. Do you want to lengthen the person's life at the risk of decreasing his or her quality of life? When considering treatments, including medications, remember that Alzheimer's disease is ultimately a fatal disease.

## Hospitalization

Hospitalization can be very difficult for people with Alzheimer's. Find out whether care can be provided on an outpatient basis or at home.

- If hospitalization is unavoidable, speak to the staff members about your loved one. This may be helpful if some staff are unfamiliar with the nature of Alzheimer's disease. Provide the staff with a written list of important information about your loved one. Advocate for your loved one's needs but try not to overwhelm the staff with too many demands.
- Try to have family or friends available as much as possible to answer questions from the staff and to reassure your loved one. Make sure you have breaks and take care of yourself, too.
- See if a private room is an option. Bring familiar items to the room, such as pictures of family and favorite quiet music.
- You may need to ask specifically for the services of a social worker who can help answer your questions, advocate for your loved one and plan for discharge. Social workers are trained to help you communicate with the hospital staff and maneuver the various professional networks involved in caregiving.
- Check with the doctor about how long your loved one may be expected to stay in the hospital. Ask for a daily update on the discharge date. If you receive conflicting information from various doctors and nurses, ask your social worker to help you clarify the information.
- Make sure you communicate with the hospital staff about your goals for care, quality of life, mood and pain management.

## Explaining the disease to children

Families may choose to protect young children from the knowledge that a grandparent or other relative has Alzheimer's disease. But children often recognize when something is wrong. Your loved one's behavior may seem frightening or disturbing, especially if the children don't understand why that behavior is occurring. Here are some ways to help you involve and support young children during this time:

- Children may need help to understand what's happening. Share information about the Alzheimer's diagnosis using terms they can understand. This will help the children cope emotionally with the personality changes that occur in the person with Alzheimer's.
- Children may feel scared, confused, embarrassed, angry, sad, lonely or guilty. Reassure them that your loved one can't help the way he or she is acting. It's not the person's fault, and it's not the children's fault.
- Children may have many questions: Will I get this disease? Is Grandma crazy? What will happen next? Try to answer the questions honestly and with as much reassurance as possible.
- Draw out worries and concerns by asking the children about any changes they've observed in your loved one. Help them imagine what it would be like to have the disease. Ask for their opinions about how you might improve care.
- Prepare the children for later changes that may occur as the disease progresses, such as language problems, difficult behavior and inability to perform the activities of daily living.
- Watch for signs of withdrawal, impatience, poor school performance, headaches, stomachaches or other minor ailments. This may signal that a child is having difficulty with coping.
- Give the children suggestions for interacting with your loved one: "Grandma has a hard time understanding us now, so we need to be gentle and speak slowly and quietly to her."
- Provide activities for both the children and your loved one to

enjoy together, such as reminiscing with a photo album, listening to music or stringing Cheerios to hang on a tree for the birds.
- Use books and videos to facilitate and enrich your discussion with the children. The local Alzheimer's Association chapter may be a good source of these materials.

## Planning for the holidays

You may wonder how to plan for holiday seasons when your loved one has Alzheimer's disease. If your loved one can't partici- pate in large family gatherings, should gatherings be held at all? Should you modify traditions? Consider the following as you pre- pare for celebrations:

- Try to set realistic expectations for you and your loved one. As a caregiver, you probably won't have the time or energy to participate in all the activities you once did. Your loved one probably won't be able to handle lots of stimulation.
- Caregivers may feel pressure to do things, visit people or trav- el when they really don't want to. Participate only in what you feel comfortable doing. Concentrate on having a nice time with the people you love. Don't be afraid to enjoy some quiet time by yourself or attend events without your loved one.
- It's easy to feel guilty if a loved one can't take part in every fes- tivity. Families may try to over-involve a loved one. Actually, by limiting and simplifying the activities your loved one is involved in, you're looking out for the person's best interests.
- Prioritize which traditions are most important to you and which you can live without.
- Simplify your holiday preparations:
    - A home-cooked meal at your house might still be an option if you ask people to bring potluck.
    - Try to limit baking, for example, by making two or three kinds rather than a dozen varieties.

- To make things easier, consider a photocopied holiday letter rather than individually handwritten cards.
- Modify traditional activities to include your loved one at his or her current ability level:
  - If attending religious services is overwhelming for your loved one, have family members alternate attending early or late services with staying at home. Sing festive songs and read inspiring passages with the person at home.
  - Do holiday baking together. Have your loved one measure flour, stir batter, roll dough into balls or simply watch as you work. Use favorite recipes and ask for advice.
  - Reminisce about favorite holiday memories.
  - Compose messages for this year's cards or holiday letter with your loved one.
  - Sing holiday songs together or guess the names of tunes on an instrumental tape.
  - Have a child read favorite holiday stories or religious verses aloud.
  - Take a drive around town to look at seasonal decorations.
  - Wrap gifts together or have the person attach tags or bows.
  - Read through the cards you receive with your loved one. Reminisce about the people who sent them.
- It may be easier for your loved one to attend small, short gatherings throughout the season rather than one big party.
- If you do have a large family gathering, reserve a quiet room for your loved one to relax in. Keep track of the stimulation from music, television, conversation and meal preparation. If it's getting too noisy, tone things down or encourage your loved one to rest in the quiet room.
- Prepare visitors for your loved one before they arrive. Send a letter or make a phone call to update them on behavior changes since their previous visit. Provide tips on how to interact with the person.
- People with Alzheimer's get worn out easily as the day progresses — a condition sometimes called sundowning — so consider having your holiday meal earlier in the day.

- Mingle your loved one's usual routine with seasonal activities. Completely changing the routine or altering the look of the environment with decorations might confuse the person.
- Avoid setting out candies and other edible decorations or artificial fruits and veggies, which might be mistaken as snacks. You may want to forgo using blinking lights on the tree or in windows since they can increase confusion.
- Avoid holiday shopping with your loved one during evenings and weekends since these are the times when stores are most crowded. You might choose to avoid stores altogether and instead pick out gift ideas from a catalog.
- Deciding whether to take a loved one away from a nursing home during the holiday is difficult. Try a small outing before the holiday to see how it goes. Think about how last year went and how the person's impairment has progressed since then.
- Some people in nursing homes feel anxious when they are away from their familiar environment. In that case, having small family groups visit for 1 or 2 hours throughout the day or preferably over several days might work best. Be sure to provide periods of rest between the visits.
- Some caregivers hold a large holiday dinner at home, choosing to visit the loved one at the nursing home some time that day. Then, on the next day, they bring the loved one home for a smaller gathering and a dinner with leftovers.
- Consider joining holiday activities planned by the assisted living facility or nursing home.
- Throughout the holiday season, expect to feel varying emotions. The holidays can be as painful as they are pleasurable. Be prepared for some post-holiday letdown. Your fluctuating emotions are normal. Try to work through them by taking a break or by sharing your emotions with a friend or support group.

## Telling others about the diagnosis

Caregivers often wonder whom to tell about the diagnosis of Alzheimer's disease and when to tell them. This may be a frightening time for your loved one. You may be torn between wanting to protect your loved one's dignity and wanting to share what you're going through. Consider the following suggestions:

- If your doctor did not inform your loved one of the diagnosis, your first decision may be what to tell your loved one. Consider his or her level of impairment. If you don't think your loved one would understand the diagnosis or you suspect he or she would be unable to cope due to impairment, you may choose not to reveal the results. You may also describe the diagnosis as a problem with memory or a memory disorder rather than using the words *Alzheimer's disease*.

- If your loved one is mildly impaired and has been told of the diagnosis, try to include the person in deciding whom to inform.

- Start the process by creating a list of those people who could most likely support you if informed of the diagnosis. A strong support network is an important part of caregiving. People are less likely to offer assistance if they don't know what is wrong.

- Notifying neighbors may be particularly important. They'll be more likely to contact you or offer your loved one assistance if they notice unusual behavior or if your loved one seems lost.

- Consider writing a letter with specific information about the diagnosis and the signs and symptoms your loved one is presently experiencing. Include in the letter how you anticipate the disease will effect your lives in the future and specify in what ways people can be supportive.

- Often, the more clearly you describe your needs, the more likely people can provide help. For example, you might say, "We are always looking for people to drive us to doctor appointments or help with yard work."

- Be sure to include your own needs as well as those of your loved one. Even if your loved one can no longer directly engage in conversation, you may still appreciate visitors who can give you emotional support or hands-on assistance.
- Think about writing an update every 3 to 6 months to keep friends and family up-to-date on you and your loved one's condition. Your local Alzheimer's Association chapter can provide you with written material about the disease process that you might include.

## When a person can no longer drive

Driving and Alzheimer's always make for a risky combination. A person who receives a diagnosis of the disease will eventually need to stop driving. It's usually better to stop sooner than later. Rarely will your loved one voluntarily choose to surrender the car keys. The decision generally falls to the caregiver. Here are a number of considerations to help you make this decision and some tips to ease the transition for your loved one:

- You might begin by keeping a written record of any changes in your loved one's driving behavior.
- You or your doctor can contact the state department of motor vehicles to request that your loved one take a driver's test. Some states require physicians to report diagnoses of Alzheimer's disease to the department.
- Your loved one may need to be informed of the decision to stop driving. Remember, however, that Alzheimer's disease affects the ability to reason. Don't spend too much time trying to convince the person why he or she can no longer drive. A simple statement may be best.
- Driving is a symbol of autonomy. Giving up the car may be a tremendous loss for your loved one. Allow time to grieve. Acknowledge the emotions your loved one is feeling.

- When your loved one asks to drive, avoid giving a straightforward no. Tell the person you would like to drive, you're taking a new route, he or she deserves a rest or the doctor doesn't recommend driving because of a heart condition or other illness.
- Out of sight may mean out of mind. Park the car where your loved one can't see it. Hide the keys, and if the person enjoys carrying a set of keys, provide substitutes that don't work.
- Your loved one may continue to enjoy rides in the family car. If a familiar vehicle prompts the person to want to drive, however, you may want to sell the car and replace it with a different make and model. Your loved one may be more likely to allow someone else to drive if the car is unfamiliar.
- Ask for assistance in learning how to disable the car. Older-model cars may be easily disabled by removing the distributor cap. A mechanic may be able to install a kill switch that must be deactivated in order to start the car. And, of course, you can always disconnect the battery.
- If your loved one has a particular mechanic, be sure to alert that person in case your loved one asks for help in getting the car started.
- Substitute a photo identification card for a driver's license. This ID can be obtained through the department of motor vehicles.
- Look for alternative means of transportation such as senior buses, taxis and public transportation. Arrange for family members and friends to give rides. Check with your local Area Agency on Aging or Alzheimer's Association to learn about transportation options in your community.
- Keep in mind that as Alzheimer's disease progresses, your loved one will likely feel less need to leave the safe, familiar home environment. Eventually, for example, it will be easier to run errands for your loved one rather than providing transportation to the store.
- Use a caregiver support group to help you cope with your own reaction to your loved one's inability to drive and to receive additional suggestions for getting the person to stop.

GUIDE

## When a person can no longer live alone

How do you know when a person should no longer live alone?
There is no clear answer. It will be different for every family. You
know the situation better than anyone else. Rely on your instincts,
but don't be afraid to ask for the help of family, friends and professionals who can assist you. You'll need lots of support. Here are
some general guidelines:

- Watch for warning signs in the behavior of your loved one.
  These safety concerns may signal that he or she can no longer
  live alone:
    - Does the person feel anxious, lonely or afraid to be alone?
      Is the person wandering away from home?
    - In the kitchen, does the person leave the stove burners on
      or food sitting out on the counter? Is food in the refriger-
      ator fresh and well covered?
    - Is the person taking medications reliably?
    - Do you notice odors or incontinence?
    - Does the person dress appropriately for the weather
      when leaving home?
    - Would the person know what to do in an emergency?
    - Are the person's physical, emotional and social needs
      being met?
- Consider the health and well-being of the primary caregiver.
  Determine whether additional in-home resources could relieve
  stress and help meet the needs of your loved one.
    - Utilize caregiver support groups.
    - Consider whether family members or friends are avail-
      able to provide hands-on assistance in providing care.
    - Professional services may exist that provide in-home
      help. Locate these services through your local Area
      Agency on Aging or the Alzheimer's Association.
- Some caregivers wait for a crisis before looking for alternative
  housing options. Your loved one's health and your own health

are both unpredictable. Don't let a crisis make your plans for you. Find out what resources exist in your community before you need their services.

- Admitting your loved one to a nursing home or assisted-living facility may become unavoidable if:
    - Your loved one has a need that requires skilled medical care, such as a hookup to an IV or oxygen, wound care or frequent injections.
    - Your loved one breaks a hip or becomes bedridden.
    - The primary caregiver becomes physically or emotionally unable to provide care due to burnout, illness or death.
- Admitting your loved one to a nursing home or assisted-living facility may have benefits including:
    - Staff who are trained to provide personal care, activities and nursing needs.
    - Relief from providing daily care, which allows you to spend more quality time with your loved one.
    - The opportunity for your loved one to socialize with other people.
    - Time for you to meet your own non-caregiving needs. When you take care of your own needs, you have more energy to focus attention on your loved one.

## When a person can no longer manage money

Because the disease causes impairments to memory, judgment and reasoning, Alzheimer's makes people vulnerable to financial abuse. Your loved one may give away or spend large sums of money, or may not recognize if someone is taking advantage of his or her finances. To protect your loved one's assets, consider the following:

- Find out your state's laws about becoming a financial conservator or guardian. Or try to find a trusted relative or a professional to serve in this capacity.
- Make sure someone is keeping a close eye on account balances. Is your loved one withdrawing large amounts of cash or writing a lot of checks? Alert someone at the bank about the diagnosis and ask that this person contact you if he or she notices suspicious activity.
- Keep watch for signs that your loved one may be purchasing large quantities of the same item or stowing cash in hiding places around the house.
- Eventually you'll need to limit or remove your loved one's access to cash, bank accounts and financial decision-making. This should be done when you notice your loved one is confused about balancing checkbooks and paying bills or is exercising poor judgment in spending.
- Most people with Alzheimer's feel more secure if they continue to have a few dollars in cash in their wallets or purses. You can provide your loved one with a small amount of cash, but don't give the person more than you feel comfortable losing.
- Contact your local Area Agency on Aging, Alzheimer's Association or caregiver support group for assistance in taking over financial matters.

## When a person can no longer work

Work is a way we contribute to our society and connect to our world. Work may be integral to our understanding of who we are as individuals and supports our sense of self-esteem. Some people with Alzheimer's are able to continue working for a short time with assistance. Choosing to no longer work and end a career may be a painful process, particularly for younger people with the disease. The following ideas may help your loved one through this time.

- Think about informing the employer as soon as possible if your loved one has received a diagnosis of Alzheimer's. Ask whether work tasks may be simplified or work hours decreased. Your loved one may find it easier to phase out employment rather than quit abruptly.

- Your loved one may have mixed feelings about telling co-workers about the diagnosis. But telling others increases the likelihood they'll provide assistance as needed. Offer to be with your loved one when co-workers are told. If appropriate, stay in touch with co-workers and keep them informed of any new developments.

- Maintaining a consistent routine can help your loved one continue to function without relying heavily on memory skills. Try to arrange a work schedule that doesn't fluctuate dramatically.

- Remember that Alzheimer's affects judgment, planning, reaction time and problem-solving skills. Consider whether the job requires making decisions that could jeopardize the safety of your loved one or of others. See if it's possible for your loved one to be reassigned to easier tasks.

- When your loved one is no longer able to work in the current setting, it may cause a loss in self-worth and identity. Try to be supportive during this time. Acknowledge painful feelings. Reassure your loved one by discussing the person's importance in your life.

- Identify ways to bolster your loved one's sense of accomplishment and contribution to society. Look for other activities he or she can participate in. Encourage your loved one to engage in household tasks by asking him or her for help: "You are such a good worker, Mom. I'd love your help folding these towels."
- Try out elder care programs in your area. Your loved one may be able to attend a center during regular work hours and participate in activities in a community setting. Many caregivers find it helpful to frame this time as "going to work."
- Watch for signs of depression as work skills deteriorate. These signs include changes in appetite and sleep patterns. Other characteristic signs are excessive crying and anger. Share any concerns with your doctor.
- Accept support from your family and friends during this difficult time. Ask for help when you need it.

# Common medical concerns

## Dehydration

People with Alzheimer's may forget to drink enough fluids and become dehydrated. Dehydration can increase confusion, dizziness, constipation or diarrhea, fever and a rapid pulse.

- Encourage your loved one to drink plenty of fluids, generally around eight glasses of liquid a day. This can include water, tea, coffee, juice or milk.
- Keep a glass of water or a favorite beverage near your loved one throughout the day. Provide gentle reminders — for example, by asking, "Does your juice taste good?" or "Is your water cold enough?"
- Beverages containing caffeine may increase anxiety and sleeplessness. If you choose to decrease your loved one's caffeine intake, phase out caffeinated beverages slowly or else symptoms of caffeine withdrawal, such as headaches, may occur.
- If your loved one was accustomed to drinking coffee throughout the day, try serving cold beverages in a coffee mug.
- If incontinence is a problem, you may not want to encourage drinking fluids after dinner. However, don't discourage fluids altogether because of incontinence. This may cause dehydration, bladder infections and other complications.

## Pain

Although Alzheimer's disease may not cause pain, your loved one can experience pain from many other sources, including stomach cramps, pressure sores and sprains — and even tight-fitting clothes. Problems arise as your loved one loses the ability to tell you in words what's hurting him or her.

- Watch facial expressions and body language for signs of pain. For example, wincing, grimacing or pulling away sharply from touch may indicate your loved one is uncomfortable.
- The person may be unable to indicate where pain is occurring. Use bathing and dressing times to look for swelling, redness, bruising and other signs of pain or injury.
- Sometimes complaints of pain may indicate emotional distress such as depression, boredom or fatigue.
- Talk to your doctor about a pain management regime that is safe for your loved one.

## Bladder Infections or Urinary Tract Infections

A urinary tract infection (UTI) often occurs when bacteria are present in the bladder or the urethra, the tube that transports urine from the bladder. Under normal circumstances, the bacteria are flushed out during urination.

- A UTI may cause pain when urinating, fever, increased confusion, blood in the urine and fatigue.
- Consider the possibility of a UTI if your loved one experiences a sudden change of behavior, such as increased anger, confusion or drowsiness.
- In late-stage Alzheimer's disease, UTIs are a leading cause of death. This is because the body is unable to fight off infection when the person becomes bedridden.
- If you suspect your loved one has a UTI, your doctor can perform a urine analysis to look for the presence of harmful bacteria. A UTI is generally treated with antibiotics.

## Falls

Some studies have shown that people with Alzheimer's will experience at least one fall during the course of the disease. They're also twice as likely to experience a hip fracture than people their age who don't have Alzheimer's.

- Physically restraining your loved one may not prevent falls from occurring and may actually increase the likelihood of injury. Some falls may not be preventable.
- Your loved one is not likely to remember to call you for assistance when he or she wants to get up, even with frequent reminders. Try putting a sign on a lap tray that says, "Stay in your chair. I'll be right back."
- Have your loved one sit on the edge of the bed for a few moments before trying to stand.
- Bedrails are metal structures raised alongside beds to prevent falls. The use of bedrails is controversial. Some people believe bedrails can prevent their loved one from rolling out of bed or from standing up and falling. However, people with Alzheimer's have been known to climb over bedrails and fall or to injure themselves after becoming stuck between the rails. Your state may have guidelines regarding the use of bedrails. Also, you may be asked to indicate your preference to a nursing home.
- In case of a fall, try to remain calm. Sit with your loved one to determine if an injury has occurred. Look for signs of redness, swelling, bruises or broken bones. If you believe a bone is broken or a head injury has occurred, call for emergency medical assistance. If your loved one seems uninjured, eventually encourage the person to stand independently rather than trying to lift him or her.
- If you do try to lift your loved one, put your hands underneath the armpits and use your legs for strength rather than your back.  Try to have a neighbor or family member ready to

call on for assistance. Remember that you'll not be able to care for your loved one if you become injured.

- Clear walkways of clutter and keep them well lit. Use carpet tape to secure rugs to the floor. Consider installing handrails along stairways and halls. Have plenty of nightlights in place to guide the person after dark, especially to the bathroom.
- A physical therapist can help determine whether your loved one could benefit from the use of a walker or other device and what type would best fit his or her needs.
- Grab bars, non-slip decals and walk-in showers will help reduce the likelihood of falls during a bath.
- Changes in the color or texture of flooring may cause falls. For example, dark spots in a carpet or tile pattern may be perceived as holes by a person with Alzheimer's.
- Contrasting colors may help your loved one locate the toilet and bathtub more easily. For example, it may be easier to distinguish the toilet and tub if they are a dark color and the floor is a light color than if all the fixtures and the floor are white.

## QUICK GUIDE

### Dental Care

People with Alzheimer's may neglect dental hygiene and develop oral infections. Poor dental care can also affect nutrition.

- Tell your dentist about the diagnosis of Alzheimer's. Some dentists have more experience working with people with dementia than do others. Ask a support group for referrals.
- Make sure the dentist is aware of all medications the person is taking. Some medications can cause dry mouth or other conditions that could affect dental health.
- Help your loved one brush after each meal. Your dentist may be able to provide dental aids such as mouth swabs that can be used in place of a toothbrush. Ask your dentist for suggestions if your loved one is refusing to open his or her mouth.

- Give simple one-step instructions for brushing teeth: "Take the cap off the toothpaste. Good, now squeeze the tube. Good, now brush your top teeth."
- Brush your own teeth at the same time to model the process.
- Help your loved one grip the toothbrush by attaching a bicycle handle or aluminum foil to the handle of the toothbrush. Or try using a Velcro strap around the person's hand and tucking the toothbrush inside the strap.
- If you are helping your loved one brush, use a spoon to gently pull the cheek away from gums to help you see the teeth.
- Encourage eating raw fruits and vegetables at meals. Also, suggest rinsing the mouth with water after meals, particularly if the person has difficulty brushing teeth.
- Some caregivers choose to no longer have their loved one use dentures as the disease progresses, and so they provide the person with a soft diet. A dietitian can help you meet the specific needs of your situation.
- Refusing to eat is often a clue that a person has mouth sores or poorly fitting dentures. Ask your dentist for assistance.

## Pressure Sores

Pressure sores may occur if your loved one sits or lies in the same position for several hours at a time. Bones can wear away at muscle and skin when the body is not regularly readjusted.

- A warning sign that your loved one is beginning to get pressure sores is red and swollen skin, particularly at places where the body is in contact with a chair or bed. Seek medical assistance if you are concerned about a suspicious spot on the skin. Eventually the red areas may become open sores, exposing the bone, if not treated.
- Common locations for pressure sores include knees, elbows, hips, heels, shoulders, shoulder blades, spine, buttocks and

ankles. Make sure your loved one does not lie on any spot that is developing a red color.

- If your loved one is sedentary, reposition him or her in order to reduce pressure on certain parts of the body. Try to do this about every 2 hours. Place pillows between the knees and ankles when the person is lying on his or her side. Use foam or gel pads to cushion vulnerable areas.

- Engage a home health agency to help you provide personal care and to move your loved one. Ask staff in the nursing home how often your loved one is being repositioned throughout the day and night.

- Poor nutrition or ill-fitting clothes can put people at further risk for pressure sores. For example, make sure clothes are comfortable and adequate in size.

## Choking

If your loved one has difficulty eating or swallowing, inadequately chewed food may become lodged in the throat or windpipe. Your loved one will be in danger of choking. Most often, solid foods such as meat are the cause.

- A universal sign for choking is a hand clutched to the throat, with thumb and fingers extended. The person's face will assume a look of panic, the eyes may bulge and he or she may wheeze or gasp.

- While eating, try to make sure your loved one's head is tilted slightly forward. Leaning back may make the eating difficulties worse.

- Use soft, thick foods to ease the process of swallowing. If you put foods in a blender, use a product called a food thickener, which is tasteless and helps to even out the food texture. For example, if you blend strawberries, the fruit may separate into pulp and liquid, increasing the likelihood of choking. Using a thickener will smooth the texture of the strawberries and make swallowing easier.

- Be prepared for emergencies. Ask a nurse or your local Red Cross for techniques to help your loved one if he or she is choking. Be ready to use these techniques if your loved one can't breathe, talk or cough.
- For more information on assisting a loved one who is experiencing difficulty eating, see the Quick Guide section on eating and nutrition.

# Part 4

*Caregiving for Alzheimer's disease*

# Chapter 8

# Becoming a caregiver

A caregiver is anyone who takes responsibility for the needs of another person, either permanently or temporarily. This may include medical care and physical care as well as companionship and emotional support. The caregiver may be required to make important treatment decisions, enlist medical services and represent a loved one's interests. At the same time, a caregiver must carefully tend to his or her own mental and physical health. There may be other responsibilities, including a career and parenting.

Explaining every aspect of the caregiver's role is beyond the scope of this book. The appendix "Additional Resources" can direct you to more in-depth caregiving information. What this and the following chapters provide are basic guidelines to caregiving.

## Initial steps

If a family member receives a diagnosis of Alzheimer's disease, you may feel overwhelmed at first. Give yourself time to let the diagnosis sink in. You may have a variety of emotional reactions to the news, including sadness, disbelief, anger and guilt. Once you have allowed yourself time to absorb the diagnosis, you may begin the process of becoming a caregiver. Here are some initial steps you can take:

## Gather information

Educate yourself about Alzheimer's so that you can understand the disease process and find creative ways to cope with its symptoms. Talk to your doctor and other health care professionals. Read as much literature as you can on the subject. Information can help you plan for the future and adjust to changes the disease will bring to your relationship with your loved one.

---

### The Alzheimer's Association

The Alzheimer's Association is a nonprofit organization dedicated to providing support and education to people with Alzheimer's, their families and their caregivers. The association was started over 20 years ago by family members of people with the disease. The Alzheimer's Association has chapters all over the country. To find the chapter nearest you, contact the national office at 800-272-3900 or at *www.alz.org*.

---

### Prepare to make health care decisions

If your loved one is able, this may be the time to talk about his or her wishes about health care. Is longer life preferable to quality of life? If a treatment may prolong your loved one's life but is accompanied by pain, immobility or dissatisfaction, should the treatment be used? A document known as a living will can be filled out, specifying your loved one's preferences for cardiopulmonary resuscitation (CPR), tube feedings and other medical treatments. You can ask your local Area Agency on Aging for referral to a professional who can assist you in filling out a living will.

### Prepare legal documents

As soon as possible, make sure your loved one has completed legal documents appointing durable power of attorney to a trusted friend, family member or professional. *Durable* means the appointment remains valid after your loved one is no longer competent to make decisions. Most states have similar laws regarding the process, but these laws may not transfer from state to state. The power of attorney for health care gives the appointed person the right to make important health-related decisions on behalf of the person who is sick. These decisions include the legal right to place an individual in a nursing home or assisted-living facility. The power of attorney for finances allows the appointed person to sign checks, sell property and handle all other financial matters.

## Revealing the diagnosis to others

You and your loved one may struggle with whom to tell about the diagnosis. You may wish to protect your loved one's privacy and wonder what people will think about the news. Your loved one may not want to feel "under the microscope," with people closely watching for signs of the illness. But as the disease progresses, hiding the diagnosis becomes increasingly difficult since cognitive and behavioral changes become more apparent.

When other people are aware of your situation, they're more likely to lend a hand, particularly if you provide information about your specific needs. The diagnosis can also help explain the behavior of your loved one, which may otherwise confuse, bewilder, embarrass or anger unknowing onlookers. Neighbors are more likely to alert you if they see your loved one wander from home. For more assistance, see "Telling others about the diagnosis" in the Quick Guide.

## Providing support in social situations

Reassure your loved one in social settings by staying close by and stepping in when he or she is unsure of what to do. Review names before attending a gathering or give your loved one prompts by saying, for example, "You remember our neighbor Joe from across the street." Some caregivers also carry a card that reads, "The person with me has Alzheimer's disease. Thanks for your patience." This card can be shown to cashiers, waiters and others to explain your loved one's behavior without embarrassment.

Some people with Alzheimer's may feel smothered by overprotective caregivers. Assess how much assistance your loved one may require and try not to exceed that assessment. Also recognize that no matter how much or how little you do, a person with Alzheimer's may not be satisfied — and you may get the brunt of that dissatisfaction.

## Changing roles and responsibilities

When a loved one is experiencing cognitive impairment from Alzheimer's, a family member or friend will likely be responsible for making decisions, providing basic care and meeting personal needs. These responsibilities can create major changes in the existing relationship and can cause a reversal in roles. Initially, spouses may feel uncomfortable about assuming responsibilities once held by their partners. Children may hesitate to decide personal matters for a parent. You may struggle to balance the checkbook or cook a meal if that had never been a responsibility before. Some changes are more personal and may require difficult emotional adjustments.

As awkward and uncomfortable as you may feel, you must recognize that all people with Alzheimer's disease eventually need someone to step in and provide care. Even if your loved one seems resentful or angry with your help, you're doing what the disease demands of you.

---

### Intimacy

If you're caring for a spouse with Alzheimer's disease, your sexual relationship is likely to change. Your loved one may experience either an increase or a decrease in sex drive due to effects of the disease or of its treatment. At the same time, you may experience changes in sexual desire toward your spouse as you take on caregiving responsibilities. Your part of the relationship may feel more parental. You may also be uncertain if your loved one is capable of consenting to sex. Go slowly and use your instincts to determine whether the experience is pleasurable for both of you. If either partner is uncomfortable with the experience, it should not happen.

Regardless of how much impairment your loved one is experiencing, touch is a powerful tool for communicating affection and reassurance. Touch can be experienced in many ways, including holding hands and hugging. When used during conversation, touch can indicate that you see and hear your loved one and you care about what's being said.

# Impact on family and career

As you transition into a caregiving role, you may find other aspects of your life receiving less attention. There's less time and energy to share with your family or direct toward your career. Rather than feel guilty or trapped by this change, try finding ways to integrate all aspects of your life. Be open and honest about your situation and look for support where it's offered.

## Your family

Consider having regular meetings to update family members about your loved one's condition and the challenges both of you currently face. Provide family members with an opportunity to help out if they're willing to do so. Create a list of your loved one's needs and work with your family to delegate tasks. Be open about the disease with young children and teenagers. Involve them in plans to support your loved one as much as they feel comfortable.

Recognize that as the primary caregiver, you generally have the best understanding of the situation. Listen closely and respond to family questions, but at the same time, make sure your voice is heard. A good rule of thumb is to assign decision making in proportion to the amount of time someone spends with the person with Alzheimer's. For example, if a wife cares for her husband 90 percent of the time, she should have 90 percent of the decision-making power.

Some families find it helpful to meet with a social worker, psychologist, nurse or other professional who has specific knowledge about Alzheimer's disease. These specialists can assist you in planning for the future, identifying needs and making decisions. To locate a professional who specializes in Alzheimer's, ask your doctor for a referral or contact your local Alzheimer's Association or Area Agency on Aging.

**Overcoming denial.** Most family members will want to be supportive, but some may experience denial about the diagnosis or minimize the impact of the disease on you and your loved one. Denial is a natural reaction to painful news and can be a form of protection in difficult situations. However, remaining in denial may ultimately be harmful, particularly when it prevents your family from supporting you. Family members in denial may question your judgment and discourage you from using essential resources. Try to share information with them, but recognize that you may never be able to convince them about the realities of the disease.

Something that may help is to share your doctor's written report that details your loved one's diagnosis. If you haven't received a report, ask for one from the doctor's office. If you keep a journal, you may want to share entries that describe specific disease-related incidents. The best way to convince people in denial about Alzheimer's disease is to have them spend more time with the loved one.

**Long-distance support.** Even if you live far away from the primary caregiver, your support can be critical to his or her ability to cope. Stay in frequent contact by telephone or e-mail. Send cards and letters of support. Try to visit and offer some respite if that would be helpful. Learn about the disease by reading and attending local classes or support groups. Ask the caregiver to inform you about situations where he or she could use assistance and try to find local resources to meet those needs.

The most important way in which you can support the caregiver is to avoid passing judgment on his or her decisions. Try to listen closely and ask questions about the situation. Don't assume you know what's happening. Your emotional support, love and encouragement can be integral to the way in which this journey unfolds.

### Your career

Young adults or spouses caring for someone with early-onset Alzheimer's may need to negotiate around the demands of a career. You may feel torn between wanting to focus on your loved one and attending to your job. Some caregivers are able to set up an alternative work schedule with their employer by cutting back on hours, by job sharing or by taking a leave of absence. Talk with your employer and see what options may be available.

If you're thinking of leaving your job, try to consider the ramifications of this action. On the one hand, quitting your job may include the loss of income, benefits and security, as well as the loss of your sense of identity. On the other hand, staying with your job may be difficult if you can't arrange alternative care.

While on the job, you may worry continually about your loved one and deal with sleep deprivation. Consider all of the resources that your community might offer to help care for your loved one while you work. Placing your loved one in an outside-the-home facility may be a better solution than leaving your position.

## Dealing with your own emotional and physical reactions

Alzheimer's disease is usually as challenging for the caregiver as it is for the person with the illness. Your loved one may eventually lose the perception that there is a problem, but you will continue to see your loved one's decline. You may find your life revolving completely around the needs of your loved one.

These changes and responsibilities can tax your body and soul. At times, you may feel frazzled and overwhelmed. It's normal for caregivers to be frustrated and even angry toward the person who has Alzheimer's. Rather than being overcome by guilt because

### Warning signs when you may need help

As you spend time caring for your loved one, you may lose sight of your own needs. Caregivers are at high risk of depression, physical illness and fatigue. Watch for these signs that you may need help.

Do you:

- Easily lose patience with your loved one?
- Find no joy in any aspect of life?
- Get angry with your loved one?
- Experience a lack of sleep?
- Care for your loved one 24 hours a day, 7 days a week?
- Feel despair, anguish or depression?
- Experience changes in appetite or energy levels?
- Often drink or use drugs?
- Have frequent crying spells?
- Think about suicide?

Seek help from a professional if you're experiencing any of these challenges.

of these feelings, try to recognize them as normal. Find healthy outlets for releasing these emotions. Share your feelings in a safe setting, for example, in a caregiver support group or with an understanding friend. Go for a power walk, punch a pillow or have a good cry. But try not to direct your reactions at the person with the disease. The disease is causing the changes in your loved one's behavior — and your loved one has no control over the behavior.

Thinking for two demands most of your attention. It's hard to maintain the energy you need if you're not getting enough sleep, ignoring your own physical needs and spending every waking hour thinking about Alzheimer's disease. If you want to be available to provide care, you may need to find ways to receive a respite from your caregiving responsibilities. Without regular breaks, you'll likely burn out, become ill or lose the ability to positively affect your loved one's care.

## What will happen if you can no longer provide care?

Caregivers often worry about what will happen to their loved one if they are unable to provide care due to illness, injury or death. A good thing to do is to be proactive and explore your options early.

- Talk with your family to help you create a plan.
- Talk to local care facilities to find out if you can have an application and other paperwork on file for quick admission.
- Find out if your local care facilities will provide short-term respite care if you become ill or need surgery.
- Keep a house key with someone you trust who doesn't live in your home.
- Look into programs that will give you a bracelet with a call button in case you experience a medical emergency.
- Try to find a senior center that has a program in which you are called once a day to make sure you are well. Or arrange to touch base with friend at the same time every day.
- Make a list of important information that an emergency caregiver would need to know.

By taking care of yourself, you are taking care of your loved one. Here are some ways to sustain your physical and mental health:

- See your doctor for regular checkups.
- Rest, eat well-balanced meals and exercise regularly.
- Find a way to have a 2-hour break at least twice a week. Spend part of that time in an activity unconnected to Alzheimer's disease.
- Share your experiences with a support group, friends or family.
- Monitor your use of alcohol and medications.
- Watch for signs of depression and seek help if you need it.
- Try to maintain a sense of humor and continue to do things you enjoy with or without your loved one.

With good support, respite and self-care, your caregiving journey can become an easier process.

## Finding support

To take care of your personal needs throughout the caregiving experience, you may need to call on various sources of support. Support falls under two categories: informal and formal.

Informal support refers to friends, family, neighbors and faith communities. These groups often consist of people who knew your loved one before onset of the disease. They may be very reliable when you need to arrange respite care. And their home visits can be as much for your benefit as for your loved one's by keeping you socially connected. However, some caregivers report that although these groups are well-meaning, they sometimes drift away, leaving the caregiver feeling hurt and confused — and without the promised help.

How can you maintain a connection with your informal support systems? Inform them of your situation and be specific. Through a phone call, a visit or a detailed letter, tell people about the diagnosis, the symptoms and the behaviors of your loved one. Describe your current needs for assistance and give suggestions for activities to use during visits.

Formal support systems include any nonprofit or for-profit agency that provides assistance to individuals in caregiving settings. Formal support includes home health agencies and elder care centers.

## Using your informal support system

When someone says, "Let me know if you need anything," you can give the person a list of ways he or she can help:

- Provide transportation to doctor appointments.
- Call or visit once a week.
- Send cards and letters you can read aloud.

- Help sort medical bills.
- Bring over a hot meal.
- Do laundry or yardwork.
- Ask occasionally how you as caregiver are doing.

Another approach is to list all of the tasks you're accountable for in a day. See if you can delegate some to others.

Various residential care settings may provide a place where you and your loved one can live so you can continue to be together, or where your loved one can live in a community setting with others experiencing similar conditions. Options might include nursing homes and assisted-living facilities. To locate resources in your community, contact your local chapters of the Alzheimer's Association and the Area Agency on Aging.

Finding systems of support is not something to do only if you have the time or when you reach a crisis. Engaging long-term support is critical to sustaining your health and the well-being of your loved one throughout the disease process.

# Chapter 9

# Day-to-day care

As your loved one experiences the changes brought on by Alzheimer's disease, he or she will require increasing amounts of assistance from you. You may ultimately be "on call" for your loved one 24 hours a day, 7 days a week. The activities of daily living, such as eating, dressing, maintaining personal hygiene, taking medications, cleaning, shopping, paying bills and providing transportation, may eventually become your full responsibility. That's a lot for one person to manage! You may also become the primary emotional support for your loved one, who will watch you for cues that indicate how to react or what to do next.

Although you can't control the course the disease takes, you can shape the way in which you provide care and the way you cope with the responsibilities. The more you understand how Alzheimer's disease affects cognition, behavior and communication, the better you'll be able to help guide your loved one through the disease process and have a positive impact on the experience. Disease-related changes will seem less mysterious, and you may find it easier to respond.

## Adjusting your expectations

To meet the demands of caregiving, it's important to have realistic expectations of your loved one's needs and of what care you're able to provide. You will likely be the central person in your loved one's life. You can provide high-quality care, but you may need to be ready to adjust, willing to acknowledge some limitations and anticipate a few missteps.

Having realistic expectations of your loved one's abilities and behaviors makes the experience easier for everyone. For example, imagine that your loved one becomes confused and puts shoes on the wrong feet. If you respond by saying, "What are you doing? You've put your shoes on wrong!" your loved one may withdraw. If you frame your response in a way your loved one can understand, the experience may be positive. For example, gently explain that you'd like to see the shoes so that you can polish them and then help put them on the correct feet.

Of course, you can't hope to protect your loved one from hurt feelings in every situation. There will be moments of misunderstanding and tension. Try to view these moments in the context of your expectations. Learning from your experience can help you prepare for future changes, which in turn may make it a bit easier to guide your loved one through this journey.

## Assessing independence

In the early stages of Alzheimer's, your loved one may still be able to perform common tasks that he or she habitually did for many years. Some of these tasks, such as managing money and driving a car, are the elements that allow a person to live and function independently. Inevitably, though, as the disease progresses and cognition progressively declines, these responsibilities will no longer be possible. At some point, probably sooner rather than later, your loved one will need to stop or be eased out of these responsibilities.

You're in a position to observe the daily experiences of your loved one and to monitor the changes in cognition, behavior and ability. You may want to keep a notebook in which you record these changes and other events of significance. This can help you track the progression of the disease and respond to questions from your doctor and other health care professionals. Because your loved one will not be able to accurately answer questions about symptoms and changes, doctors will often rely on you to provide information. As well, your insight may be the critical factor in deciding when your loved one should cease activities such as driving and taking care of finances.

## Working

Some people in an early stage of Alzheimer's are able to continue working with assistance for a short time. Eventually, they will need to leave their jobs. It will be important to create a plan that allows your loved one to leave with dignity.

Initially, you'll need to determine whether he or she wants to continue working and whether he or she still possesses sufficient judgment and problem-solving skills to do so. Furthermore, you'll have to decide whether it's still safe for your loved one to continue. Consider how to share the diagnosis with the employer. Discuss with the employer whether job hours could be cut back and job tasks simplified to a manageable level.

Retiring from a career can be painful. Jobs contribute to a person's sense of self-esteem, identity and involvement in the world. If you or the employer feels your loved one can no longer continue, try to find an alternative or an avocation that gives your loved one some of the same feelings associated with work. For example, a sense of "habit" is less likely to be impaired by the disease than is short-term memory. It may be helpful to at least maintain the hours of a work routine to whatever extent possible. So, for instance, if your loved one previously went to the office at 8 a.m., you might leave the house together around that time and go for a cup of coffee.

Try to provide reassurance and encouragement to your loved one during this transition. Perhaps you can compile a scrapbook with highlights of his or her work life, filled with pictures, notes from colleagues, and mementos. No matter what type of career your loved one had, emphasize the difference his or her life has made in the world. For more tips, see "When a person can no longer work" on page 148.

## Managing money

Eventually, your loved one will lose the ability to balance a check-book, pay bills, do taxes and handle other financial matters. You may discover overdue notices or bills that have been paid several times. Make sure someone reliable has been appointed with durable power of attorney (POA) for finances. This individual can monitor bank balances and check with bill collectors to make sure your loved one is handling money appropriately. If not, the person with the POA will have to take responsibility for these areas. Your loved one is vulnerable to financial abuse, so be sure to alert his or her banker, attorney and anyone else who can help watch for unscrup-ulous behavior on the part of others.

Some caregivers feel uncomfortable or reluctant to assume finan-cial responsibility for a parent or another family member. At these times it's important to remember that you still have your cognitive functions although your loved one may not. It's essential that you step in to help even if the disease prevents your loved one from rec-ognizing this need.

When possible, involve your loved one at an appropriate level with financial transactions. For example, you can have your loved one fill numbers into a blank bank book as you pay bills. If this is too difficult for your loved one or is upsetting, find other activities that are less disturbing. For more tips, see "When a person can no longer manage money" on page 147.

## Driving a car

Do you remember how great it felt to drive a car by yourself for the first time? Driving is deeply connected to a sense of independence. And among the most difficult decisions caregivers face is deciding when a loved one is no longer able to drive safely. It's no wonder that families struggle with the decision to take away the car. As one daughter said, "It's the last thing my dad can do by himself."

Some caregivers choose to allow their loved one to drive only in familiar neighborhoods or only when the caregiver is riding along. This doesn't adequately address how your loved one will respond if an unexpected detour arises or a child darts into the road. Other caregivers employ a wait-and-see method, saying, "He hasn't had any trouble up till now, so we're keeping our fingers crossed." If this is your plan, ask yourself what sign you're waiting for. Minor accidents may be definite signs for you to intervene, but a major accident could happen before a minor one.

Remember that driving is a privilege and not a right. Alzheimer's disease impairs judgment, planning, visuospatial skills, reaction time and insight, all of which are essential to maneuver a ton of steel down the road. Families who wait too long to take away the car risk injury and death, not only to their loved one but also to others. Most experts in Alzheimer's disease feel it's important to help the person stop driving as soon as possible after a diagnosis has been made. A rule of thumb is to ask yourself whether you would ride in a car that your loved one was driving. If the answer is no, then you know it's time to take away that privilege.

## When is it time to stop driving?

Observe your loved one's driving habits for signs of potential trouble. You should probably intervene right away if you notice any of the following changes:
- Failing to yield
- Getting lost
- Problems with changing lanes or making turns
- Driving at inappropriate speeds
- Confusing the brake pedal and the gas pedal
- Being confused about directions or detours
- Hitting the curb while driving
- Forgetting to use turn signals
- Driving recklessly

When you decide it's time to stop your loved one from using the car, stay committed to your decision. It's not your fault that your loved one should no longer be driving — blame Alzheimer's disease. You're simply ensuring your loved one's safety. Try to find ways to help your loved one stay active and feel useful and capable.

Decide how you're going to tell your loved one about the decision to stop driving. Try to elicit the support of family, friends and neighbors. Your doctor may be willing to fill out a "no driving" letter or to accept the blame: "The doctor says you can't drive any more." Recognize that your loved one will also need time to grieve and adjust to the loss. Try to remember that although those feelings may be directed at you, they're actually about the disease.

You may decide not to tell your loved one about the decision. Some families remove the car without discussion and offer always to do the driving. A simple explanation such as "Your car is at the mechanic's shop" may suffice. If you do discuss the decision, recognize that you're not likely to convince your loved one of the need to stop driving. Provide a simple answer and then respond to the person's emotions.

Even if you initially tell your loved one about the decision, you may need to find clever ways to prevent your loved one from driving. This may entail removing the keys, parking the car around the block or disabling or selling the car. For more tips, see "When a person can no longer drive" on page 143.

### Living alone

All people with Alzheimer's disease will eventually lose their ability to live alone safely. If your loved one lives alone at the time of the diagnosis, you may need to decide at what point to change living arrangements. This can be one of the most difficult transitions for families to make throughout the entire disease process. As you make this decision, try to involve other family members, medical professionals, and people involved in your loved one's day-to-day existence. For tips, see "When a person can no longer live alone" on page 145.

If your loved one lives in a well-populated area, you may be able to arrange for in-home services to provide some assistance. If these services aren't available, you may be the one responsible for all aspects of care. Or you may need to change the living arrangement and move your loved one from his or her home.

If you decide to make a change, one of your options may be having your loved one come to live with you or a family member. This option deserves a careful, objective assessment before it's enacted. Private time with your immediate family will diminish, and finding a safe haven away from caregiving duties may be next to impossible.

Sleep deprivation is common for caregivers living with their loved one. You may become frustrated and have difficulty hiding your feelings. Make sure you have a support network. You might consider respite for short-term breaks.

If you decide not to live with your loved one, it doesn't mean you love him or her any less. You're choosing to let others help you provide care so that you can focus on other aspects of your relationship. You may consider admitting your loved one to an assisted-living facility or a nursing home.

## Behavior changes

One of the most difficult aspects of Alzheimer's disease is coping with changes in your loved one's behavior. Many people with Alzheimer's feel anxious and worried. Some may become agitated and try to wander away. They may ask for a person who is no longer living or talk about going to school today as though still a student. Some may experience aggressive behavior and strike out at others. Many people with Alzheimer's ask to "go home" even if they still live in the same house. Of course, the behavior changes will be different with each person.

Many behaviors are directly related to memory loss. For example, if your mother asks for a parent or wants to go to school, it's probably because she's forgotten that her parents have died or that she's an adult who no longer attends school. Be patient and respond to her emotions. Try to be reassuring and not to argue or convince. It's far more likely that if you try to bring her back into reality, your mother may become upset or simply not believe you. For more information about behavior changes associated with Alzheimer's, see "Challenging moods and behaviors" on page 111.

### Join, validate, distract

There are various ways to respond to the behaviors exhibited by people with Alzheimer's. One way is the ABC method described on page 72. Another is to join the person's reality, validate how the person is feeling and distract the person with another activity.

Generally, it's best to join your loved one's reality and respond as though you believe what's said is true. Then give an explanation that makes sense in the context. For example, you might tell your mother that her parents have gone to visit relatives or that there's no school today because it's Saturday. This may make you feel like you're lying. But with the reality changes in your mother's mind, the goal should be to comfort her however you can. Frame your response in a way that she can understand. Some caregivers refer to this concept as therapeutic fibbing.

The emotions your loved one expresses are very real, even if the reasons behind these emotions aren't logical. Some people in the early stages of Alzheimer's disease report that they feel as if people no longer take them seriously. Show your loved one that you're listening by making eye contact and giving feedback. Validate feelings by acknowledging you recognize the emotions.

Help your loved one focus on something positive by finding an activity to distract his or her attention elsewhere. If your mother is upset because she thinks she needs to go home and care for her young children, for example, you can join her reality and acknowledge how upset she is. Give her an explanation that makes sense — for example, the children are at a birthday party and won't be home for several hours. Then distract her with an activity such as baking cookies or listening to some favorite sing-along music.

## Communication

Your loved one's ability to communicate with language will decrease as the disease progresses. You may have difficulty understanding what your loved one says. You also may find it difficult to speak to your loved one in a way that he or she can comprehend. Either of these situations can frustrate your loved one and lead to agitation and even aggression.

Your approach to communication should include patience, understanding and the ability to be a good listener. Use familiar words and simple concepts. Speak clearly and directly to your loved one. Use visual cues such as pointing or demonstrating, and don't hesitate to repeat what you've said after a moment if your loved one doesn't respond.

Behavior often becomes the way people with Alzheimer's communicate their feelings and needs to others. To understand a behavior, consider what it may be communicating. If your husband is asking to go home, for example, imagine what home may symbolize for him. Home is often associated with comfort, familiarity, safety and belonging. Can you find other ways to help him feel that way? Paging through a book of old photos while wrapped in a familiar blanket and holding hands, for example, can give some of the comforts of home. Pacing might mean your loved one is tired,

## When do you correct someone with Alzheimer's?

Sometimes your loved one will say things that are incorrect. The statement may be minor, such as the wrong date or season. Other times, the mistake may be more disturbing. Perhaps your husband tells a visitor that you never let him leave the house. When do you try to correct your loved one? How do you let other people know that a statement is incorrect?

First ask yourself, what's the primary goal in providing care? Most caregivers want to help their loved one experience feelings of acceptance and reassurance rather than insist upon the absolute truth of a situation. You may try a gentle correction, but pay close attention to your loved one's response. If your dad laughs and says, "Oh yes, that's right," then it's not a big deal to provide the correction. If he doesn't believe you or becomes angry, then the correction is doing more harm than good. And even if your dad isn't bothered by corrections, you may simply grow tired of giving constant reminders. Ask yourself, does it really matter?

You may also wait to correct or clarify the misstatement with others until you're out of your loved one's hearing range. A subtle shake of your head can help set the record straight. Most people probably realize your loved one is confused. If the incorrect statements are being made during a doctor visit, write down your observations and ask for time alone with your doctor.

feels hungry or needs to use the bathroom. A bit of detective work can help you determine what the behavior is saying.

Some people may find interacting with your loved one to be frightening or painful. Generally, the more information they have about the disease, the more at ease they may be during a visit. You may need to provide visitors with tips on how to communicate with your loved one before they arrive. For example, if they try to converse, suggest that they try straightforward yes-or-no questions rather than quizzing. You might also suggest specific activities that can ease the interaction. This might include looking at a coffee-table book together or reminiscing about the past.

## Environment

The environment can have a definite impact on your loved one's behavior. If a noisy room seems overwhelming, shut off the television and limit background noise to quiet music without commercials. If your loved one seems agitated by groups of visitors, try to limit their number at gatherings. Encourage visitors to call before they come. If you or your loved one is having a bad day, don't be afraid to reschedule a visit. You may want to encourage short visits to avoid overwhelming your loved one.

When outside the home, you may find it easier to avoid large, loud settings such as amusement parks or places with many young children. Familiar destinations may be easiest for your loved one to feel relaxed. Try not to cram too many activities into a single trip. Plan for rest periods between activities and locate a quiet haven for your loved one to retreat to if necessary. For more tips, see "Travel and transporting outside the home" on page 107.

The environment can also be confusing. A long hallway with lots of doors may be baffling to someone looking for a place to nap or use the bathroom. Give cues to help your loved one navigate the space. Consider using arrows made of masking tape on the floor, pointing the way to special places. Put a sign on the bathroom door with a picture of a toilet. Put a picture of your loved one as a younger person on the bedroom door. (The picture can indicate a personal space for someone who has trouble reading.)

The most important aspect of the environment is how it feels. Help your loved one feel welcome, safe and comfortable. Be accepting no matter what changes the disease brings. Scolding or reprimanding won't help. Gently guide rather than push your loved one when you want to change a behavior. Remind yourself that it's the disease, not the person, causing the changes.

## Activities of daily living

Frustration, agitation and even aggression can occur when people with Alzheimer's have difficulty doing tasks that once came easily. As you and others help your loved one with eating, bathing, grooming, dressing and going to the toilet, find ways to make the experience less frightening and frustrating for both of you.

Take your time helping your loved one with personal care tasks. He or she may have difficulty remembering all of the steps involved in dressing or brushing teeth. Trying to rush things will just add to the confusion and slow down the process. Go slowly and break down tasks into simple steps.

Try to stay with the same routine your loved one has utilized in the past. Did your mom always bathe and dress before breakfast? Or take a sponge bath in the evening? Staying with the familiar schedule can make the process easier for both of you. Of course, everyone has good and not-so-good days. Try to be flexible and go with the flow if she isn't comfortable with a task at the usual time.

Involve your loved one in tasks as much as possible. Some people can still choose an outfit if given only two choices, rather than a closet full of clothes. Your loved one may be able to use a toothbrush if you start the motion. If nothing else, have your loved one hold an object while you provide care.

Make sure your loved one's dignity is being preserved as much as possible. Keep doors shut during dressing and bathing. If the person perceives mirror reflections as other people in the room, cover the mirror with a towel or curtain.

If a particular task is always frightening or upsetting, try to distract your loved one by singing a favorite song, telling a story or joke or providing a snack. Sometimes, though, distractions may provide too much conflicting stimulation for the person. Use your own discretion. More than likely, you'll need to try a variety of approaches to find what works today. And what works today may not work tomorrow. Have patience with your loved one and with yourself. You are forging new territory in your relationship. For more tips, see "Activities of daily living" on page 95.

# Chapter 10

# Planning long-term care

I t's extremely difficult, if not impossible, to be the sole care provider for someone with Alzheimer's through the entire course of the disease. Eventually, there will be times when you may need some form of assistance, even if it's only for one task or for a few hours a week. Depending on where you live, a variety of care resources may be available to help you.

One obstacle you may need to overcome in getting this assistance is your own reluctance to ask for help. You may be worried that your loved one won't feel comfortable with other caregivers. Maybe you think that no one else can provide care as well as you can. These reactions are common and may be, to some extent, valid.

In fact, getting assistance can make caregiving less burdensome, both physically and emotionally. This assistance can provide other resources and skills that you may not possess and give you a chance to rejuvenate your caregiving. Your loved one may actually seem to improve when these other resources are used. This can occur because his or her socialization has increased. The improvement can also relate to your lowered stress level as a caregiver.

## Introducing your loved one to a new care arrangement

When you use a new resource, you are indeed letting go of some control over your loved one's care. Although the care from others will be different, your influence can make a big difference. You know your loved one best. Don't be afraid to share your insight.

When you introduce your loved one to the new situation, try to project a positive attitude. Help your loved one feel safe and secure with the new experience. You might introduce an in-home caregiver as a nurse or just a new friend. You might describe going to an elder care center as going to work or going to stay with friends.

Provide the staff with information about your loved one's personality, life story, routines and common challenges. After helping your loved one settle into the new situation, allow the staff to take over.

You may find it helpful during the initial visit to stay close to your loved one and the new provider. Your presence may be reassuring as they get to know each other. When it's time for you to leave, plan how to proceed ahead of time with the new caregiver. You may excuse yourself to run errands, go to a doctor's appointment or simply say, "I'll be back soon." You may also decide to slip out without saying goodbye to avoid calling attention to your absence.

### Information that other care providers may need

You can help other care providers by making them aware of:
- Your loved one's routine
- Important events from his or her life story
- Common concerns your loved one has and how best to handle them
- Preferences for activities, music and snacks

# Living arrangements

Any new care arrangements you make will involve blending the needs of your loved one with your capabilities as a caregiver. What kinds of tasks do you require help with most? Is it bathing and feeding your loved one, or cleaning the house, doing yardwork or running errands? Do you still work outside the home or have other, noncaregiving responsibilities to attend to? Regardless of your situation, remember that caregivers generally perform better with several hours of respite every week. Here are several different types of professional care that may be available in your community.

### Home health services
Home health services vary from one organization to the next. The most common assistance involves personal care such as bathing, dressing and grooming, and helping your loved one with eating and going to the bathroom. Some agencies also provide help with meal preparation and household chores. Most provide different levels of nursing care, including assistance with injections, wound care and medical equipment. Some agencies may also provide physical therapy.

Generally your relationship with an agency starts with a home visit by one of the agency's social workers or registered nurses to assess your needs. Arrangements for payment may be discussed at this time.

### Elder care programs
Elder care programs are designed to provide socialization and activities for adults in need of assistance. Some programs are specifically designed for people with Alzheimer's disease. Others are simply for older adults. Some centers may also accept people with developmental disabilities, including mental retardation. One of these programs may meet your needs.

Elder care programs are generally open during daytime hours, usually weekdays only, and offer a variety of services. Most will provide a lunchtime meal and lots of activities. Some offer transportation from your home to the center. You may find centers that even offer to give your loved one a shower during the visit. Of course, you can choose whether or not to accept any of these services.

Elder care programs can be a wonderful opportunity for your loved one to spend time engaged in activities with other adults, such as cooking or baking, playing games, singing, watching movies, and doing arts and crafts. You may wonder if your loved one would enjoy such an experience and would like being around a group of new people. The answer isn't always easy to gauge, but you may be pleasantly surprised at what your loved one finds enjoyable, even as the disease progresses.

### Alternative housing

There may be a variety of alternative housing options in your community. Some housing may consist of little more than apartment buildings in which older adults live independently. Other housing may have amenities such as communal dining or visits from a nurse or home health aide.

Assisted-living facilities (ALFs) are another option. ALFs are designed for people who need help with personal care and require general guidance but who don't need the specialized medical care of a nursing home. ALFs generally have shared or private bedrooms, shared living quarters and shared dining and kitchen areas, and staff available to assist the residents. Often, residents of ALFs spend more time in community living spaces than in their bedrooms and many of these homes have planned activities.

Ideally, the staff will have training in dementia caregiving techniques. Make sure to inquire about staff availability. Most people with Alzheimer's can't learn a call system, so you will want someone to check in on your loved one frequently and provide assistance with activities of daily living and meal preparation. You may also want to check how much time residents spend in community settings during the day.

### Nursing homes

Nursing homes are designed for people who need skilled medical care. These facilities may be a good choice for individuals who need injections, IVs or wound care, who are bedridden, or who are in a wheelchair. Nursing homes generally assist with meals and personal care and organize activities and socialization.

Some nursing homes have special units for people with Alzheimer's disease. Sometimes these units are really just a part of the regular nursing home, but they occupy an area set aside for people with Alzheimer's. Other units have been designed so that the environment, activities, philosophy of care and staff training revolve around the special needs of people with Alzheimer's.

### Hospice

Hospice services are available for people in the last stages of life. A doctor's order is necessary to access these services. For more information on hospice, see page 197. To learn about hospice services in your community, talk to your doctor, social worker, nursing home staff or a local Alzheimer's Association chapter.

## Additional services

Programs that offer respite and support also may be available in your community. These services can make a big difference in your ability to provide effective caregiving.

### Respite

Respite services offer care for your loved one as a means to give you, the caregiver, time off from your duties. Time off can mean several hours in an afternoon or overnights, weekends and weeklong vacations.

Respite may be available through a variety of informal resources. For example, family, friends or neighbors may be available to help. Some communities have in-home volunteers or professional caregivers to provide respite. These services may be contacted through the Alzheimer's Association, Area Agency on Aging, in-home health agencies or even churches.

Assisted-living facilities and nursing homes may offer short-term stays, particularly if they have empty rooms available. You may need to plan your breaks at the last minute depending on room availability, but this can be an excellent way to get time off. Respite can also help your loved one get accustomed to a new living arrangement before moving in. And respite may actually delay long-term placement if these short stays help refuel your energy.

## Safe Return Program

People with Alzheimer's may become easily disoriented as the disease progresses. The Safe Return Program, administered by the Alzheimer's Association, is designed to assist people who are at risk of wandering away from home and getting lost.

When you join the Safe Return Program, a file is maintained in a national database with identifying information, a photograph of your loved one and contact information for you and other family members or friends. If your loved one is missing, you can call a toll-free number to file a report. The registry will fax the identifying information and photograph to local authorities.

The Safe Return Program also provides identification bracelets or pendants. Your loved one's bracelet indicates his or her first name, the words "memory impaired," an identification number and a toll-free telephone hot line number. Your bracelet identifies you as a caregiver and includes an identification number and hot line number. If someone finds your loved one in need of assistance, the person can call the hot line number and a Safe Return operator will contact you. If you become incapacitated or unable to communicate, your bracelet can inform someone that you're a caregiver and your loved one may need assistance.

Talk with the Alzheimer's Association for more information about the Safe Return Program. Find your nearest chapter of the Alzheimer's Association by calling 800-272-3900.

## Support groups

A support group consists of caregivers in similar situations who meet to share their experiences and emotions. Meetings are generally facilitated by a professional or by a trained volunteer. Attending a support group can be an opportunity for you to hear from others who have dealt with issues similar to those you experience. There may also be times when you aren't looking for new ideas or advice — you just want to be among people who understand what you're going through.

With more emphasis being placed on the early diagnosis of Alzheimer's disease in recent years, support groups for those with early-stage Alzheimer's are becoming more common. To join, generally your loved one must have some recognition of the diagnosis and must want to talk to others who are dealing with similar experiences.

To find support groups in your community, contact the Alzheimer's Association or the Area Agency on Aging. Some groups may be specifically for Alzheimer's caregivers, while others may encompass broader caregiving issues.

## Online support groups

You may find a variety of chat rooms and e-mail support groups on the Internet. Be cautious of information you receive from these sources. What you find may not be reliable. Use your own good judgment about the Internet and check advice with a trusted medical professional.

## Finding the best care arrangement

To enlist resources from your local community, you may want to start with two of the nation's largest Alzheimer's referral services: the Alzheimer's Association and the Area Agency on Aging. You can also contact your local department of human services or department of social services for referrals. Their telephone numbers should be listed under "County" in the government section of your phone book. Also check the Yellow Pages under the various care options. A local senior citizens center may have an advocate or social worker, either of which can provide referrals.

### Assessing your needs

Spend time thinking about the types of assistance you currently need and the assistance you'll likely need in the future. It may be helpful to prioritize your needs in a list, from most helpful to least necessary. Try to match the resources in your community with the needs you listed. If you can't find a professional service to meet your needs, talk to family members, friends and neighbors, or community leaders.

## Needs checklist

If I could receive help as a caregiver in one area, would it be:
- Meal preparation?
- Household chores, such as cleaning and laundry?
- Neighborhood errands to shops or the post office?
- Personal care, such as bathing and dressing my loved one?
- Daily care during my work hours?
- Skilled medical care for my loved one?
- Respite from caregiving?
- Financial planning?

Have your list available to show friends when they say, "Let me know if there's anything I can do to help."

Try to use more than one resource. For example, you can plan for your loved one to go to elder care on Mondays and Thursdays and to receive a bath from an in-home health aide on Tuesdays and Fridays. Your son can come to cook dinner once a week, and your daughter can have your loved one stay at her house one weekend a month.

### How to evaluate quality of service

The way in which a professional caregiver interacts with your loved one can have a profound impact on care. As you gauge the quality of care, try to strike a balance between serving as your loved one's advocate and not overwhelming the staff with too many minor concerns. Keep in mind that you may be limited as to how much control you have over certain issues, such as which room your loved one occupies or the staff-to-resident ratio. Try to identify how various issues impact your loved one's experience and be willing to let go of those that have a minimal effect.

At the same time, it's important for you to be included in decisions that ensure that your loved one's needs are met. The best way to make this happen is to keep the lines of communication open. Offer your input as a team member and reassure the staff of your desire to be part of the team. Approach staff members in a gentle, assertive manner and be prepared to listen to the reasons behind a particular approach.

## If you're concerned about the quality of care

Before addressing your concern with a care provider, ask yourself:
- Does this issue really matter?
- Who will this issue bother?
- Is my loved one at risk of physical harm?
- How dramatically will my loved one's quality of life improve if this issue is addressed?

For example, if your father lives in a nursing home and he and his roommate often wear each other's clothes, who is this practice bothering? On the other hand, if your father becomes aggressive during bath time when in the care of a particular staff member, by raising this concern, you can help defuse the situation.

Determine the organization's chain of command and the appropriate person you should go to with concerns. A specific issue can probably be addressed to one caregiver, whereas a concern about the overall care plan should be addressed to the management team. If you have a substantial concern and don't get results, work your way up the chain of command.

## How to know when a change is necessary

Your loved one's safety and well-being are of primary importance. If you're seriously concerned about either, you may need to find a new agency or institution to assist you. If you have grave concerns about a specific care provider, seek help immediately. Report signs of physical, emotional or financial abuse to the proper authorities.

There's an advocacy organization that investigates concerns about care providers in each state. To contact your state's ombudsman — a public official appointed to investigate your complaints — look in the phone book or check with the Area Agency on Aging or Alzheimer's Association. You can also call your local department of social services to contact a social worker who works in adult protective services or with vulnerable adults.

## Assessing your financial situation

The costs associated with caring for a loved one with Alzheimer's disease can run high. The Alzheimer's Association reports families spend an average of close to $175,000 throughout the course of the disease. Personal savings, investments and property can be sources of income to help meet these costs. You or your loved one may also be eligible for various financial services that will help defray expenses. It's vital for you to be aware of these sources.

When preparing for the financial aspects of care, consult with a financial planner, an attorney who specializes in estates or a knowledgeable accountant about payment plans for care alternatives. Find out how much money can be gifted to family members, how much money the spouse can keep and how best to utilize the financial resources available to you.

---

### Finance checklist

The following information about your loved one may be necessary as you prepare to assess the financial options for care:
- Bank accounts and credit card accounts
- Will
- Insurance policies including those for life, health, homeowner, auto and long-term care
- Retirement benefits including pensions, annuities, Social Security, IRAs or Keogh plans
- Stock and bond certificates
- Real estate deeds and mortgages
- Vehicular titles
- Consumer loans and outstanding debts
- State and federal income tax records
- Safety deposit boxes and keys
- Social Security and Medicare numbers
- Contact information for lawyers, accountants and insurance agents

Adapted from *Alzheimer's Disease: Legal and Financial Facts You Should Know*, the American Health Assistance Foundation, 1998.

Before meeting with the person, compile all of the important information about your loved one's assets (see "Finance checklist"). Consider potential expenses associated with care, including medical appointments, prescription medications, care services and supplies. Work with your financial consultant to create strategies for handling investments and assets and to identify financial resources.

If you plan to use a care option such as home health services or an alternative living arrangement, payment may be discussed before enrollment. Ask the agency which payment options are available. Each care option may have specific requirements regarding which payment sources they'll accept.

## Financial services

Financial services that may be available to assist you include health insurance, retirement benefits, veterans benefits, tax credits and special programs through the Social Security.

### Health insurance options

Government-funded insurance such as Medicare and Medicaid — known in some states as medical assistance — and private insurance are among the financial options you may use to pay for medical care and services.

**Medicare.** Medicare is a federal health insurance program for people 65 and older who are receiving Social Security benefits. The program covers some costs associated with Alzheimer's disease, including portions of diagnostic procedures as well as follow-up visits and inpatient hospital care. Under specific circumstances — when your loved one requires skilled care for a condition that is capable of improving — Medicare will cover home health services, physical therapy, medical supplies and equipment, and medical social services. Medicare will also cover many hospice costs. Medicare does not pay for elder care or respite care, prescription drugs, incontinence supplies, vitamins, or nutritional supplements.

Medicare will pay for up to 100 days of nursing home care but, again, only under special circumstances. Your loved one would have to have been an inpatient in a hospital for at least 3 days in

## Receiving full Medicare benefits for a loved one's diagnosis

Medicare will pay 80 percent of the costs associated with evaluating and diagnosing your loved one for Alzheimer's disease. But when you receive medical statements, you may discover that Medicare has only paid 50 percent of the costs. Why the discrepancy?

Doctors bill the diagnosis of Alzheimer's disease under different diagnostic codes. Alzheimer's disease is code 331 and is covered at an 80 percent rate. Depression (code 311) and presenile dementia (code 290) have older codes and are covered at a 50 percent rate.

When doctors bill Medicare, they list the primary diagnosis first and any secondary diagnoses following. In order to receive 80 percent coverage by Medicare, the doctor must list Alzheimer's disease as the primary diagnosis. If, for example, the doctor diagnoses depression at the same time as Alzheimer's disease, which is common, and lists depression, not Alzheimer's, as the primary diagnosis, you will have only 50 percent of costs covered.

Medicare reimbursement can be complicated and difficult to understand. Check with your local Area Agency on Aging to see if there are community programs to help you deal with the bills. If you believe you haven't received full reimbursement from Medicare due to billing codes, talk to your doctor's business office.

the last 30 and now must require skilled care daily for the same condition for which he or she had been hospitalized. Meeting these specifications can be difficult, and most people who apply do not receive the full 100 days of coverage. Medicare will also pay for hospice services, which are available during the last months of life. For more information go to *www.medicare.gov*.

**Medicaid.** Medicaid is known in some states as medical assistance. The program helps pay medical costs for low-income Americans. Since Medicaid is a federal program administered by each state's individual welfare system, the benefits and eligibility requirements vary from state to state. If your loved one is eligible, most nursing home costs will be covered, along with many other medical care fees. The key question is, is your loved one eligible? It's important to plan ahead, even if you still care for your loved one at home. Check with your social services agency for more information. Also visit *www.cms.gov.*

**Private insurance.** Private insurance plans vary dramatically in scope and benefit. Some long-term-care insurance policies will pay part of the cost of a nursing home but may stipulate the reason for admission and the goal of care. For example, some policies only pay for assistance in a nursing home that is expected to improve your loved one's condition, such as treatment for a broken hip.

Talk to your insurance agent about the policies your loved one owns. Be aware that good health is often a prerequisite for obtaining a policy. Once a loved one receives a diagnosis of Alzheimer's disease, you may not be able to add any health insurance, long-term-care insurance or life insurance policies. And the earlier you enroll, generally the lower the premiums.

### Veterans Administration

If your loved one is a veteran, check with the Department of Veterans Affairs (VA) and your local VA hospital. Your loved one may be eligible to stay at a VA hospital rather than a nursing home. The VA may also help pay for up to 6 months of care in a nursing home or provide respite or family support services. Your local member of Congress can help you secure benefits from the Department of Veterans Affairs if necessary. For more information, visit *www.va.gov.*

### Tax credits

Certain expenses for care or medical treatment may be tax-deductible either for your loved one or for you, if you claim your loved one as a dependent. For example, if you work and need to use respite care, you may be able to receive a deduction for part of that cost. Certain nursing home costs that aren't covered by Medicare or Medicaid also may be deductible.

To ensure you are receiving appropriate information about tax deductions, work with a knowledgeable accountant. Contact your local Alzheimer's Association for the latest news on tax-break legislation for caregivers. Ask the Internal Revenue Service to receive a copy of the booklet *Tax Breaks for Older Americans*. For more information go to *www.irs.ustreas.gov*.

### Social Security programs

Two special programs administered by the Social Security Administration may be of assistance to you. Social Security disability benefits are available to former wage earners under the age of 65 who are no longer able to work due to disability. Your loved one must have worked 5 out of the last 10 years and needs specific documentation from a physician that confirms his or her inability to work.

Supplemental security income (SSI) provides a minimum monthly income to people who are 65 or older, blind or disabled, and who have limited assets and income. Much as with Social Security disability benefits, a physician must document your loved one's inability to work.

For more information about Social Security disability benefits and supplemental security income, contact your local Social Security Administration office or visit its Web site at *www.ssa.gov*.

## End of life

People can live with Alzheimer's disease for 20 years or more, although the average course of the disease is 8 to 12 years. Alzheimer's is rarely the primary cause of death. Rather, pneumonia, congestive heart failure or a complication associated with the debilitating effects of Alzheimer's is usually the primary cause. Much as with other stages of the disease, arrangements can be made to help you face this difficult time.

### Funeral planning

Although you may not wish to think about death, many families find it easier to make burial and funeral arrangements while their loved one is still alive. This may include arrangements for an autopsy. Such planning allows you, at the time of death, to be with your family and focus on coping rather than making difficult and expensive decisions in your grief. For assistance, contact a funeral director or, if you choose, a member of the clergy. Some financial programs, such as Medicaid, will allow you to spend a certain amount of money on prepaid funeral arrangements.

### Hospice

During the last 6 months of life, your loved one may be enrolled in hospice. Hospice assistance includes personal care, medical equipment such as hospital beds and commodes, and grief support for family members. Services may be provided in your home or in other living arrangements. Your doctor must fill out the necessary paperwork for your loved one to be eligible. Some programs are available through clinics and hospitals and others through private organizations.

In order to use hospice services, you must decide to stop any life-prolonging treatments for your loved one and focus only on comfort measures. For example, you may choose to no longer

## Symptoms of the final stages of Alzheimer's

Sometimes it's difficult for a doctor to determine when someone is experiencing the symptoms of the last stages of Alzheimer's disease. Generally the person will be bedridden and no longer able to walk. He or she may lose weight, experience seizures, have difficulty swallowing and no longer be able to speak. The person may be passive and in need of total care.

You may wonder if your loved one is aware of what's going on around him or her in this last stage of the illness. Although the body and mind are in the process of shutting down, your loved one may still be aware of your care and affection. Hold hands. Stroke his or her forehead. Say what you need to say to bring closure to your relationship. As you say goodbye, remember that Alzheimer's disease can never change the impact your loved one has made on your life and on the world.

employ ventilators, cardiopulmonary resuscitation (CPR), antibiotics and artificial nutrition and hydration (tube feeding and intravenous hydration). This doesn't mean you're providing assisted suicide. Rather, it's a planned decision not to aggressively treat medical illnesses. You can still provide pain medication and oxygen to help your loved one stay comfortable. Advance directives, including living wills and power of attorney for health care, can help you make these decisions according to your loved one's wishes.

# Additional resources

## Administration on Aging (AOA)

330 Independence Ave. S.W.
Washington, DC 20201
202-619-7501
*www.aoa.gov*

## Agency for Healthcare Research and Quality

2101 E. Jefferson St., Suite 501
Rockville, MD 20852
301-594-1364
*www.ahcpr.gov*

## The Alzheimer's Association

National Headquarters
919 N. Michigan Ave., Suite 1100
Chicago, IL 60611-1676
312-335-8700 or 800-272-3900
*www.alz.org*

## Alzheimer's Disease Education and Referral Center (ADEAR)

P.O. Box 8250
Silver Spring, MD 20907-8250
301-495-3311 or 800-438-4380
*www.alzheimers.org/adear*

## Alzheimer's Disease International

45-46 Lower Marsh
London SE1 7RG
United Kingdom
44-20-7620 3011
*www.alz.co.uk*

## American Association of Homes and Services for the Aging

2519 Connecticut Ave. N.W.
Washington, DC 20008-1520
202-783-2242
*www.aahsa.org*

## American Association of Retired Persons (AARP)

601 E St. N.W.
Washington, DC 20049
202-434-2277 or 800-424-3410
*www.aarp.org*

## American Health Assistance Foundation

15825 Shady Grove Road, Suite 140
Rockville, MD 20850
301-948-3244 or 800-437-2423
*www.ahaf.org*

## Area Agencies on Aging

(Administered by the Administration on Aging)
State-by-state index of centers:
*www.aoa.gov/aoa/pages/state.html*

## Center for Drug Evaluation and Research

Food and Drug Administration
5600 Fishers Lane
Rockville, MD 20857-0001
888-463-6332
*www.fda.gov.cder*

## Centers for Medicare and Medicaid Services

7500 Security Blvd.
Baltimore, MD 21244-1850
410-786-3000
*www.cms.hhs.gov*

## CenterWatch Clinical Trials Listing Service

22 Thomson Place, 36T1
Boston, MA 02210-1212
617-856-5900
*www.centerwatch.com*

## Eldercare Locator

(Administered by the Administration on Aging)
800-677-1116
*www.eldercare.gov*

## Family Caregiver Alliance

690 Market St., Suite 600
San Francisco, CA 94104
415-434 -3388
*www.caregiver.org*

## National Association of State Units on Aging

1201 15th St. N.W., Suite 350
Washington, DC 20005
202-898-2578
*www.nasua.org*

## National Council on the Aging

409 Third St. S.W., Suite 200
Washington, DC 20024
202-479-1200
*www.ncoa.org*

## National Hospice and Palliative Care Organization

1700 Diagonal Road, Suite 625
Alexandria, VA 22314
703-837-1500
*www.nhpco.org*

## National Institute of Mental Health (NIMH)

NIMH Public Inquiries
6001 Executive Blvd., Room 8184, MSC 9663
Bethesda, MD 20892-9663
301-443-4513
*www.nimh.nih.gov*

## National Institute of Neurological Disorders and Stroke

P.O. Box 5801
Bethesda, MD 20824
301-496-5751 or 800-352-9424
*www.ninds.nih.gov*

## National Institutes of Health Clinical Center

6100 Executive Blvd., Suite 3C01, MSC 7511
Bethesda, MD 20892-7511
301-496-2563 or 800-411-1222
*www.cc.nih.gov*

## National Institute on Aging

Building 31, Room 5C27
31 Center Drive, MSC 2292
Bethesda, MD 20892
301-496-1752
*www.nia.nih.gov*

## National Library of Medicine

8600 Rockville Pike
Bethesda, MD 20894
888-346-3656
*www.nlm.nih.gov*

## Society for Neuroscience

11 Dupont Circle N.W., Suite 500
Washington, DC 20036
202-462-6688
*www.sfn.org*

# Index

# MAYO CLINIC ON HEALTH

**Alzheimer's Disease**

**Arthritis**

**Chronic Pain**

**Depression**

**Digestive Health**

**Healthy Aging**

**Healthy Weight**

**High Blood Pressure**

**Managing Diabetes**

**Prostate Health**

**Vision and Eye Health**